The Monarch's Way

by
Trevor Antill

Book 1
Worcester to Stratford-upon-Avon
(via Boscobel)
175 miles

Meridian Books

Published 1995 by Meridian Books

© Trevor Antill 1995

ISBN 1-869922-27-1

A catalogue record for this book is available from the British Library.

Publishers' Note
Every care has been taken in the preparation of this book. All the walks have been carefully checked against the relevant definitive maps and are believed to be correct at the time of publication. However, neither the author nor the publishers can accept responsibility for any errors or omissions or for any loss, damage, injury or inconvenience resulting from the use of the book.
Please remember that the countryside is continually changing: hedges and fences may be removed or re-sited; landmarks may disappear; footpaths may be re-routed or be ploughed over and not reinstated (as the law requires); concessionary paths may be closed. The publishers would be very pleased to have details of any such changes that are observed by readers.

Maps based upon the Ordnance Survey maps with the permission of the Controller of Her Majesty's Stationery Office. © Crown Copyright.

Meridian Books
40 Hadzor Road, Oldbury, Warley, West Midlands B68 9LA

Printed in Great Britain by BPC Wheatons Ltd., Exeter.

Contents

Introduction

EVEN as a school-boy my imagination was caught by the adventure of King Charles II's escape after the Battle of Worcester in 1651. This is not altogether surprising since I was born not far from one of the scenes – Bentley Hall – and over the last fifty years my outdoor activities in the Midlands have constantly brought me into contact with this epic. Quite when the idea of a long distance walk following the royal route first germinated is difficult to say; except that it has been buzzing around for most of that time. This then is the result which should not be interpreted as an authoritative historical account, simply as an enjoyable, but long, theme walk – I am a walker not a scholar!

In researching the subject I soon realised that there were very many places where the King was alleged to have stayed, rested or passed through and not all could possibly have been so visited. There are many reasons for this, amongst them being the fact that Charles, on reaching France, deliberately created fictitious routes so as to protect those who had helped him and were still in England. The times were such that rumour and speculation was rife: in addition the King's own account – and most other people's – was not written until after the Restoration. But perhaps the reason that brings a wry re-assurance that human nature rarely changes, is the Post-Restoration realisation amongst the opportunists of the day that the 'opposition' now held the cards. This resulted in many imaginative petitions for grace and favour from those who suddenly 'remembered' the instances of their loyal assistance. This wasn't restricted simply to individuals either, whole towns and villages sometimes found it desirable to demonstrate their loyalty to the crown and the King must surely have been bewildered that he covered so much ground!

This then posed a question: how to work out a route that faithfully follows that followed by the King? I soon realised that this was not always possible; the King and his companions were often not sure themselves of the exact route taken whilst the King himself didn't always dismiss the opportunist petitions.

England's topography has also changed substantially since the seventeenth century: we have seen the advent of urban sprawl, canals, railways and motorways. Consequently I decided that the only practical solution – with two notable exceptions – was to include all places, both known and speculative, through which the monarch is said to have passed. Likewise, though following public rights of way for all but a fraction of the route, I determined not to be afraid of using modern day features such as disused railways (where permissible) and canal towpaths. The result is, I hope, a delightfully meandering long distance walk that has a fascinating sprinkle of urban history and a super abundance of outstanding natural beauty, whilst following an epoch making escape route: the difference is that you are walking for pleasure and not fleeing for your life!

The two notable exceptions I mentioned are Ombersley in Worcestershire and Whittington in Staffordshire.

Ombersley is a village about six miles north of Worcester on the A449 trunk road. Charles is reputed to have obtained refreshment at Ombersley's King's Arms (now the Crown and Sandys) whilst fleeing from Worcester. However, after leaving Worcester the King's party soon branched right from their northerly course for they found the road awash with the fleeing Scottish military. This then would indicate that Ombersley was by-passed and for this reason I have not included Ombersley on 'The Monarch's Way'.

At Whittington, the Whittington Inn is reputed to have accommodated the King overnight where he is supposed to have occupied a secret priest room. Stourbridge was the first town the king passed through and as he reached Whiteladies in the small hours of the morning it is likely that the royal party were on the move throughout that first night. As Whittington is west and south of Stourbridge then it is questionable whether the Whittington Inn was on the route. In any event it is most unlikely that Charles slept there and arrived at Whiteladies when he did.

Nonetheless, both Ombersley and Whittington are within two or three miles of 'The Monarch's Way' and diversions along the Wychavon Way for Ombersley and along the Staffs and Worcs Canal to Whittington are easily made should any reader so wish.

Since the seventeenth century the Midlands have experienced monumental changes and this stage of the route contains great diversity and contrast. From pleasant rural scenes to absorbing industrial artefacts and then back to outstanding scenery again – this book should satisfy most interests. Subsequent stages 'The Cotswolds, The Mendips and the Sea' (which book is currently in the course of preparation) and, eventually, 'The South Coast, The Downs and Escape' need little introduction as areas of outstanding beauty and interest.

In rural areas, public transport can sometimes be a problem with various local carriers providing varying services. Rather than try to quote individual timetables in each part of the country (which frequently change anyway) I have opted to quote the local Tourist Information Centres from whom local service details are available. These offices can often supply accommodation addresses as well.

Occasionally, as an aid to navigation, I have quoted compass bearings. These are always stated as Grid North rather than Magnetic North – that is, without any adjustment for magnetic variation. If you are relying solely on a quoted compass bearing, without the assistance of any other landmark, then always check it to your map – in the best regulated operation the odd error may sometimes creep in!

With a large undertaking such as this it is inevitable that, at any one time, somewhere in the country, some public footpath or bridleway will be subject to a diversion or amendment application – rather like painting the Forth Bridge it is not possible to reach a stage where everything is simultaneously complete. Where I am aware of such a proposal (which can sometimes take years to finalise) I have detailed the current definitive route and the proposed new route. In the meantime the reader should always be aware that rights of way can sometimes change and that OS maps may show an old line. Where a definitive line has been legally amended then the local authority should advertise the fact with special 'diversion' waymarks.

All that remains now is to plan your walk, enjoy the contrasts, enjoy the achievement and particularly enjoy the scenery and the feeling of history you will encounter. Good luck.

Trevor Antill

Summer 1994

Recommended Reading

There are very many books that cover the lives of Charles I, Charles II and Oliver Cromwell, and the periods of the Civil Wars and the Restoration – far too many to list here.

However, there is one book that deals exclusively with the escape of Charles II and which is highly recommended. Conveniently sized and conveniently priced it is:

The Escape of Charles II after the Battle of Worcester
by Richard Ollard.

It is published by Constable (ISBN 0-09-467280-6) and is most appropriate as a walking companion.

Along the Monarch's Way

The following places of interest and antiquity are but a few of those along the complete route of the way. The list is by no means exhaustive and does not include those places directly associated with the King's flight (which are described in the main text). While virtually all are open to, or have access for, the public it should be remembered that this is not exclusively so – more detail may be obtained from the appropriate Tourist Information Centre. All, with the exception of Stonehenge, are on or very close to the route: many more places of interest are near by.

Book 1

Harvington Hall

A moated Manor House noted for the priest holes much used by its recusant occupiers.

Hagley Hall

A Palladian style house in a landscaped park it shelters in the lee of the Clent Hills.

Stourton Castle

Though not built to any particular style the castle is primarily noted for being the birthplace of Cardinal Pole, in 1500, who became Archbishop of Canterbury after his predecessor had been burned at the stake.

Wrottesley Hall

The original Hall, built in 1696, was destroyed by fire in 1897 when certain priceless and ancient literary works were destroyed. Amongst these were a set of English Chronicles and a first set of Shakespeare. The Hall was rebuilt in 1923.

'Little Nell's Grave' – Tong

Charles Dickens stayed in Tong during the last century and acknowledged that he had the village, together with its collegiate church of St. Bartholomew's, in mind when writing the latter parts of 'The Old Curiosity Shop'. The church was the scene of a quite sophisticated Victorian 'scam' when a past verger discovered that showing people Little Nell's 'grave' was a profitable venture – an entry was even forged in the register! Today there is still a plaque marking 'The Reputed Grave of Little Nell' but alas it is quite bogus. The church itself is quite something however. Resembling more a miniature cathedral than a parish church its collection of tombs, effigies and brasses is one of the finest treasures in the country and enshrines some of the most influential of families. Since the Conquest both the manor and castle were held by many noble lines before passing to a

George Durrant II who left his mark on the parish by way of 14 children by his first wife, 6 by his second and 32 illegitimate!

Ironbridge Gorge Museum (Blists Hill)

Blists Hill Open Air Museum is part of the six square mile Ironbridge Gorge Museum – a World Heritage Site. Blists Hill is a recreated community of the 1890s set in a 50 acre site where the visitor steps back in time.

The Aerospace Museum – Cosford

This nationally famous centre is really four museums in one consisting of *The Missile Collection, The Warplane Collection, The Transport Aircraft Collection* and *The Research & Development Aircraft Collection.*

Chillington Hall

Although the present hall only dates from the eighteenth century, Chillington has been the home of the Giffard family since it passed to them in marriage in 1186. Originally three Giffard brothers came to England with William the Conqueror. The family motto, *'Prenez haleine, tirez fort'*, commemorates a formidable effort of bowmanship by one Sir John Giffard during the sixteenth century. A panther having escaped from his private collection was threatening a women and her child. As Sir John took aim his son whispered, 'Take breath, pull strong'. He obviously followed this advice for he succeeded in killing the animal. Today a wooden cross in the lodge garden marks the spot. The Giffard family's involvement in Charles II's escape is well documented.

The Black Country Museum

Another open air museum which features buildings and artefacts connected with the Midlands industrial heritage. A particularly exciting feature is the Dudley Canal Tunnel which passes through man-made limestone caverns.

The Netherton Tunnel

The last canal tunnel to be built in Britain and opened in 1858 it is perfectly straight for its 3027 yard length – the opposite entrance appears as a pin-prick of light! Cut through limestone it is surprising how quickly colourful stalactites and curtains have grown.

Halesowen Abbey

Apart from the infirmary, little remains of the Abbey itself. However, the Abbey Fishponds; a series of embankments and dams across a shallow valley; are clearly visible and little imagination is needed to see them as they would have been in medieval times. Containing probably carp and bream they would have provided an important variation of diet as well as a source of fresh meat.

Avoncroft Museum of Buildings – Bromsgrove

Yet another outdoor museum but this time with the emphasis on England's rural heritage and buildings.

The Old Malt House – Alcester

Alcester is a small market town of Roman origin, as evidenced by its name and its position straddling the Roman Ryknild Street and the River Alne. Its oldest building is The Old Malt House which dates from 1500 and is of a half-timbered, gabled construction. The Town Hall was built in 1618 and rebuilt in 1641. Most of the buildings on the eastern side of High Street were, at one time or another, ale houses! Its other old buildings and narrow streets are worthy of exploration.

Kinwarton Dovecote

In the care of the National Trust this dovecote dates back to the fourteenth century when it housed an important source of fresh meat.

Wootton Wawen Hall

Dating from the seventeenth century the hall (not open) was the elegant childhood home of Mrs Fitzherbert whom George IV, as the Prince Regent, secretly and illegally married. The outstanding village church contains aspects of virtually every style of English religious architecture.

The Obelisk – Welcombe Hill

A landmark for many miles around, it is a memorial to various members of the Philips family. This pleasant vantage point has a picnic area.

Stratford-upon-Avon

World famous as William Shakespeare's birthplace and home to the Shakespeare Memorial Theatre, this town has many other attractions to offer.

Book 2

Hidcote Manor (NT)

Celebrated and famous formal gardens set in the idyllic, thatched cottage surrounds of Hidcote Bartrim, a manorial hamlet.

The Market Hall – Chipping Campden

Built in mellow Cotswold stone, the Jacobean Market Hall must be one of the most photographed buildings in the Cotswolds. Another important centre for the wool trade upon which England was so dependent.

Batsford Arboretum

Designed and planted during the last century, the work continues today. With a strong Asian influence, the arboretum is set on the gentler eastern escarpment of the Cotswolds with good views across the Evenlode valley.

The River Windrush – Bourton on the Water

This tiny river flows through the village in an 'open plan' style under low bridges accompanied by tree-lined grassy banks. A well known Bourton attraction is its model village. A beautiful place that does become rather crowded at times.

The Almshouses – Northleach

Essentially a village since the Middle Ages its obvious prosperity emanates from the wool trade. The almshouses and the fifteenth century church being testimony to the wealth of the wool merchants. An unusual feature in Northleach is a museum (The Cotswold Countryside Collection) set in a country prison with a restored cell-block and courtroom.

Chedworth Roman Villa

A fascinating view of Roman domestic engineering set in attractive countryside.

The Norman Church – North Cerney

Set in a lovely position near the River Churn, this church is a must for those interested in religious architecture. With several unusual features from differing centuries it is something quite out of the ordinary.

The Park – Cirencester

The 3000 acre park of woodland and farms, mostly open to the public, has a five mile avenue of chestnut trees. In Roman times Cirencester was second only to London in size and importance and had three roads radiating from it. Many ancient artefacts have been discovered in the town and may be viewed in the museum. There are the remains of an amphitheatre near the town centre.

The Source of the River Thames

Which rises from a 'dry spring' in a field near Kemble!

The Sapperton Tunnel

Linking the Stroudwater Navigation to the Thames & Severn Canal, the 2¼ mile long tunnel was the longest in Britain when it was completed – though abandoned in 1933, suffering roof falls, it is still the third longest canal tunnel. The eastern portal is an outstanding piece of architecture!

The Town Hall – Tetbury

An Elizabethan market town with many fine old buildings. Its seventeenth century town hall is built on pillars set in three rows.

Westonbirt Arboretum

A Forestry Commission enterprise, the Arboretum consists of 600 acres and contains 1800 species of trees from all over the world. With seventeen miles of waymarked trails this outstanding collection can be enjoyed at any time of the year.

Horton Court

Another fine National Trust property

Dyrham Park

Owned by the National Trust, it is one of their outstanding properties famed for its tapestries and gardens.

SS Great Britain

Built by the famous Isambard Kingdom Brunel, this ship was launched in 1843 and was the first to rely mainly on propeller power. Damaged and left stranded in the Falklands, this historic vessel was towed back to Bristol in 1970 for restoration.

Clifton Suspension Bridge

Another design by Brunel, this bridge stands 245 feet above the Avon. It was completed in 1864, some five years after Brunel's death. Below the bridge is the Avon Gorge Nature Reserve.

Chew Valley Lake

A quite beautiful lake – or rather reservoir – just south of the attractive village of Chew Magna.

Wookey Hole

A celebrated group of caves formed by the River Axe which still flows through to form a lake. Occupied from Stone Age times, its obligatory and legendary witch was given some substance earlier this century when a female skeleton together with certain 'witch-like' artefacts was excavated.

The Cathedral – Wells

This world famous cathedral was first begun in the twelfth century and completed in the fourteenth. Originally adorned with almost 400 statues one of its main features are the amusingly carved pillar-capitals.

Cadbury Castle

One of the best prehistoric camps in England, the castle is believed to be King Arthur's Camelot.

Fleet Air Arm Museum – Yeovilton

A fascinating day out for the military aircraft enthusiast

Tintinhull

A pretty, old-fashioned village with the obligatory stocks. Tintinhull House is built from the local Ham Hill stone and is in the care of the National Trust.

Montacute House

Built of Ham Hill stone by the Phelips family (two Colonels of this same name were with the King during his escape!) this notable mansion is also in the care of the National Trust.

Book 3

Golden Cap

At 618 feet, Golden Cap is the highest cliff on the south coast and offers views that complement that distinction. Its name derives from the colour of the summit gravel which in certain light conditions glitters like gold!

The Pavements – Bridport

A pleasant Georgian town whose pavements were used for twisting and drying the locally made ropes, twines and cords.

Grimms Ditch

It is thought that the ditch was a pre-Roman boundary between two Iron Age communities that had differing patterns of agriculture: to the north the land was the first to be cultivated while to the south the emphasis was on grazing. The need to stop straying, coupled with the animosity that would follow, may mean that the ditch had a dual purpose.

The Price of Bread – Great Wishford

The churchyard wall records the price of bread since 1800.

Stonehenge

Less than four miles from the Way little needs to be said about this most famous of ancient sites which dates back almost 4000 years. To throw the Heale House servants off the scent the King spent a day sight-seeing at Stonehenge.

Mottisfont Abbey

A National Trust house dating from the eighteenth century and containing parts of the twelfth century Augustine priory. It contains paintings by Whistler.

The Cromwell Monument – Hursley

A Tudor village of one street, Richard Cromwell, Oliver's son, was lord of the manor here and was buried in the old church. There is a Cromwell monument in the present church. Some three miles north-east, on the very edge of Winchester, is Oliver Cromwell's Battery!

Twyford

An attractive downlands village whose main claim to fame is Benjamin Franklin who wrote part of his autobiography at Twyford House and Alexander Pope who was expelled from its school.

Open Air Museum – West Dean

Contains ancient wooden buildings taken from their sites in Sussex and Kent. West Dean itself is a lovely downlands village with flint and half-timbered houses. It also has gardens containing beech, horse chestnut and elm.

Goodwood House and Racecourse

A beautiful racecourse set high on the downs with a natural 'grandstand' in The Trundle, a 676 foot Iron Age hill fort. Adjacent is a Country Park while almost two miles to the south is Goodwood House, seat of the Duke of Richmond.

Stane Street

A Roman road dating from AD70 which runs from Chichester to London.

Arundel Castle

Home of the Earl Marshal of England the castle was built just after the Norman Conquest by Roger Montgomery. Over the centuries it has been added to, repaired and rebuilt so that today it presents a dominant, but conserved, presence over the surrounding countryside. Adjacent to the castle is a Wildfowl Reserve.

Cissbury Ring – Findon

The two ramparts of this Iron Age hill fort are the largest, and probably the most dramatic, earthworks on the South Downs. Owned by the National Trust this antiquity offers fine views over the surrounding countryside.

The Monastic Inn – Bramber

A one time provincial capital of William the Conqueror, though little remains of its castle, the village of Bramber also served as a river port for him. The timber framed, fifteenth century house – St. Mary's – is one of England's last surviving examples of a monastic inn and was originally built for the monks who were Wardens of the Bridge. It also accommodates the National Butterfly Museum.

The Royal Pavilion – Brighton

This Regency architectural orgy would not be out of place in some eastern kingdom.'What was, in its time, considered a vulgar example of bad taste has, with typical British perverseness, now become affectionately accepted.

The Marlipins Museum – Shoreham by Sea

A twelfth century building of flint and Caen stone, the museum contains historic model ships and local history artefacts as well as some fine paintings. The harbour is still a working port and privately owned.

Long Distance & other footpaths that connect with the Monarch's Way

Avon Walkway
Bath to Bristol Railway Walk
Severn to Solent Walk
Bristol Countryway
Centenary Way
Cotswold Way
Dorset Coastal Path
Dorset Downs Walk
Dorset Walk
Downs Link
Frome Valley Walkway
Heart of England Way
Leland Trail
Liberty Trail
Limestone Link
Lipchis Way
Navigation Way
North Worcestershire Path
Oxfordshire Way
Round Avon Ride
Silkin Way
Somerset Way
South Downs Way
South Somerset Cycle Route
South Wessex Way
Staffordshire Way
Sussex Border Path
Test Way
Two Rivers Way
Wardens Way
Wayfarers Walk
Wessex Ridgeway
West Mendip Way
West Midlands Way
Windrush Way (!)
Wychavon Way

Illustrations

Photographs by the author.

The Monarch's Way waymark (on the title page) and Charles II (page xix) by Jim Bray.

Sketches (pages xvii, 1, 5, 15, 32, 41, 51, 63, 87) by Norman Neasom. These are reproduced, by kind permission, from two wallcharts by Alan Richards and Norman Neasom, one illustrating the escape of Charles II after the Battle of Worcester, the other the flight of the Gunpowder Plotters. These are available, price £2.00 each, from Dr Alan Richards, 26 Ragley Crescent, Broom Park, Bromsgrove B60 2BD.

Also by Trevor Antill

Ridges and Valleys: Walks in the Midlands
Ridges and Valleys II: More Walks in the Midlands
Ridges and Valleys III: A Third Collection of Walks in the Midlands
The Navigation Way: A Hundred Mile Towpath Walk (*with Peter Groves*)

In preparation (to complete 'The Monarch's Way'):

The Monarch's Way: Book 2; The Cotswolds, the Mendips and the Sea (Stratford-upon-Avon to Charmouth) – *Publication Summer 1995*
The Monarch's Way: Book 3; The South Coast, the Downs and Escape (Charmouth to Shoreham) – *In preparation*

The Monarch's Way Association

Following the enthusiasm that has been shown towards the Monarch's Way during its planning and development stages it is proposed to establish an association for walkers, historians, visitors and others who have an interest in the walk and in the areas through which it passes.

If you would like to have more details please send a stamped addressed envelope to:

Trevor Antill
c/o Meridian Books
40 Hadzor Road, Oldbury, Warley, West Midlands B68 9LA

The Story So Far…

IT was Charles II's destiny to be born into an age of great constitutional change – an age where an increasingly strong parliament demanded greater reforms from an increasingly weakened monarchy. His father – the deeply religious and unbending believer in the Divine Right of Kings – Charles I, became more and more at odds with his parliament; a state of affairs that in 1642 inevitably led to the raising of his standard and the start of the Civil Wars.

As a healthy 12 year old boy the excitement that the young Charles must have experienced at this time can well be imagined. Initially there were some successes and the Prince, with his younger brother James, spent much time with his father and the Royalist Armies. But some two years into the war things started to change, and change for the worse, for the Parliamentarians were becoming organised. Oliver Cromwell and his 'Ironsides' became practically invincible while the Royalist forces, continually under-funded, deteriorated. Following the King's defeat at Marston Moor, and the formation of Parliament's 'Model Army', the eventual Parliamentary victory became assured.

In 1645, at the tender age of 15, Prince Charles was sent to (nominally) command the western army at Bristol. The same year the King's forces were finally defeated at Naseby.

Now there was nothing to do but flee the country. This the Prince did by joining his mother in France – his father meanwhile surrendered to the Scots who in turn, later surrendered him to Parliament. A few years of negotiation and conflict took place resulting in Charles I being executed on 30 January 1649, much to the outrage of the Scots and the Irish.

In 1650 Prince Charles left his continental exile for Scotland where a short time later the Scots army was routed by Cromwell. The following year another Scots army was raised and at its head the now crowned King Charles II marched into England to restore his inheritance. Reaching Worcester the new King learned that Oliver Cromwell had not only caught up with him, but had also intercepted his southward route.

Here, at Worcester, the final battle of the Civil Wars took place on 3 September 1651. Again Cromwell crushed the Royal Army and, at 21 years of age, Charles became a fugitive forced to flee for his life…

Charles watching the battle from the tower of Worcester Cathedral

By the Parliament

A PROCLAMATION

FOR THE

Discovery and Apprehending of CHARLS STUART, and other
Traytors his Adherents and Abettors.

Whereas CHARLS STUART Son to the late Tyrant, with divers of the English and Scotish Nation, have lately in a Trayterous and hostile manner with an Army invaded this Nation, which by the Blessing of God upon the Forces of this Commonwealth have been defeated, and many of the chief Actors therein slain and taken prisoners; but the said Charls Stuart is escaped: For the speedy Apprehending of such a Malicious and Dangerous Traytor to the Peace of this Commonwealth, The Parliament both straightly Charge and Command all Officers, as well Civil as Military, and all other good People of this Nation, That they make diligent Search and Enquiry for the said Charls Stuart, and his Abettors and Adherents in this Invasion, and use their best Endeavours for the Discovery and Arresting the Bodies of them and every of them; and being apprehended, to bring or cause to be brought forthwith and without delay, in safe Custody before the Parliament or Council of State, to be proceeded with and ordered as Justice shall require; And if any person shall knowingly Conceal the said Charls Stuart, or any of his Abettors or Adherents, or shall not Reveal the Places of their Abode or Being, if it be in their power so to do, The Parliament doth Declare, That they will hold them as partakers and Abettors of their Trayterous and Wicked Practices and Designs: And the Parliament doth further Publish and Declare, That Whosoever shall apprehend the person of the said Charls Stuart, and shall bring or cause him to be brought to the Parliament or Council of State, shall have given and bestowed on him or them as a Reward for such Service, the sum of One thousand pounds; And all Officers, Civil and Military, are required to be aiding and assisting unto such person and persons therein. Given at Westminster this Tenth day of September, One thousand six hundred fifty one.

Wednesday the Tenth of September, 1651.

ORdered by the Parliament, That this Proclamation be forthwith Printed and Published.

Hen: Scobell, Cleric. Parliament.

London, Printed by *John Field,* Printer to the Parliament of *England.* 1651.

*The text of the Proclamation offering a reward
for the capture of Charles Stuart.*

Charles II in the 1670s (after Godfrey Kneller)

Jim Bray

The Monarch's Way – the Complete Route

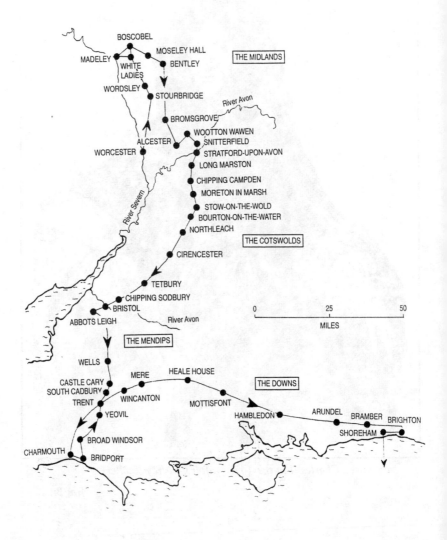

1

WORCESTER to DROITWICH

8½ miles

Following the defeat of his forces, King Charles made his way back to Worcester's Sudbury Gate – situated where the Commandery and the present day canal bridge stand – and from there to 'King Charles House'. Leaving the house and then the city, by way of St. Martins Gate, his party headed north, soon branching right to avoid the Scottish cavalry which was also fleeing in that direction.

MAPS: Landranger (1:50,000) 150; Pathfinder (1:25,000) 974 & 996.
PARKING: Public Car Parks in Worcester and Droitwich or roadside near Boycott Bridge.
TOURIST INFORMATION: Worcester (01905 726311) and Droitwich (01905 774312)
START: The Commandery, Worcester (GR 852544) or where convenient.
FINISH: Boycott Bridge, Droitwich (GR 885634)

THE START of your journey is north along the towpath of the Worcester and Birmingham Canal. Though the towpath may be accessed at several points in Worcester, one of the three following is recommended:

Firstly, Diglis Bottom Lock is the canal's junction with the River Severn. From here follow the towpath past Diglis Basin – almost an inland port – and north to bridge number 3.

Secondly, join the towpath at Sudbury Bridge – No 3. This has the advantage of being the site of the old Sudbury city gate and is next to 'The Commandery', *the King's headquarters*. Again follow the towpath north to bridge 5 where the towpath changes sides.

The Commandery, Worcester. The start of The Monarch's Way.

Thirdly, from 'King Charles House' follow the pedestrian (tourist) signs for St. Martins Gate and Shrub Hill railway station. This will bring you to bridge 5 where you head north along the towpath.

Immediately after bridge 12 you pass 'The Cavalier Tavern', a canal-side pub, and at bridge 13 the towpath changes sides again. Stay with the towpath as far as bridge 17 where you leave the canal. Cross the bridge and in a few yards go right along an enclosed path, parallel with industrial units to the right.

Follow the path as it bears left around a cricket ground and joins a road. Go left along the road – signed 'private road' but still a public footpath – and follow it between the bungalows. Beyond the bungalows continue with

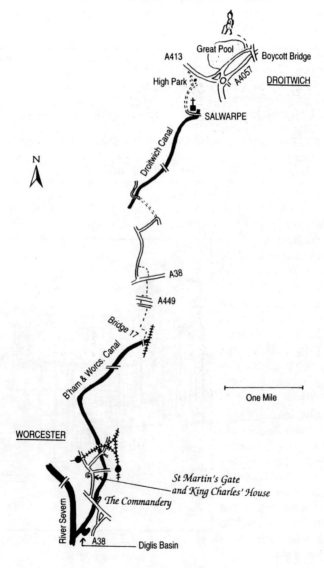

the tarmac service road with fields to your left and the industrial estate to your right. This will bring you to a T-junction with a lane just past Holy Claines Farm.

At the junction go left with the lane for about 200 yards to a gated step stile and footpath sign on the right. Cross it to then pass under the A449 trunk road. On the other side go right along the field edge, parallel to the road, for almost 200 yards. Here turn left and make a sloping field crossing (almost north – 5 degrees) to meet the opposite hedge and a gap next to a builders yard. Go through the gap and follow the hedged drive to the A38.

King Charles' House, Worcester

Turn right along the road for about 80 yards and then left along the tarmac path at the side of a children's play area. Meeting a housing estate road take the enclosed footpath between the houses opposite and then bear left with it in front of 'Lane House' flats. Continue forward to pass in front of 'Preston Court' and then across the end of a cul-de-sac to follow another enclosed path forward. This will bring you into Dilmore Lane where you turn right.

Follow the lane – signed Lower Town – for almost half a mile to pass 'Windmill Cottages' where you immediately take a right fork, again signed Lower Town. After passing a large thatched house the lane swings right. Here you go left at the sign for Hogbrook Farm and immediately left again into a hedged and unsurfaced lane. This will take you past Porters Hill Farm and down to a lane and bridge which takes you over the Droitwich Canal. Now go right along the lane that follows the edge of the canal and in about 200 yards, where they part company, follow the canal towpath which is also a right of way.

The Droitwich Canal has long been abandoned for it was rarely profitable in its prime function of carrying salt. However, at the time of writing, the Droitwich Canal Trust together with British Waterways are restoring the canal and have got as far as this point – the work being well advanced. In time it may be possible for boaters to cruise a 'Droitwich Ring' by following the River Severn, the Droitwich Canals and then the Worcester & Birmingham Canal.

Now follow the towpath for approximately 1¼ miles to enter a cutting where ahead you will see the square tower of Salwarpe church. Soon, at the start of a long brick wall on the opposite bank of the canal, you will see a path going left, down from the towpath, to pass a stile. Follow this clear path as it progresses parallel to the towpath and so reaches a step stile into a muddy paddock. Cross the paddock and exit onto a narrow lane. Turn right along the lane and quickly reach the church and Salwarpe Court.

Salwarpe Court was once a manor house and at one time was bestowed on Catherine of Aragon as part of the settlement for her short lived marriage to Prince Arthur – Henry VIII's elder brother.

In the church there is a copy of a Royal Command – dated August 1651 – whereby Charles II ordered the 'Constables and Tithingmen' of Salwarpe to bring spades, shovels and pick axes for work on Worcester's defences.

Leaving the church retrace your steps along the lane and follow it to its end where it crosses the River Salwarpe. Go through the gate in front and follow the well defined track ahead. Passing through another gate swing right and follow the track towards a white gate.

About 75 yards before the gate the definitive line of the bridleway goes left up the pasture to pass left of barns and buildings to then head north and so reach the A4133. However, this line is cut off by a gate-less fence and does not look as though it has been used for many years. At the time of writing the line in current use by walkers and horse riders alike is the route now described, though this could always change to the definitive line. Any change should be suitably waymarked.

Immediately before the white gate swing left and so arrive at another gate which you go through to then pass between brick barns left and the Jacobean farm house right – *note the remains of a moat.* A little further on the farm road goes right but you go straight ahead and through a gate into a field. In the field go left to the corner and then right to follow the edge to the A4133.

Now follows a third of a mile of road walking along the busy A4133 which is unfortunate but unavoidable. There is no pavement or verge so do exercise care.

Turn right and follow the A4133 to a large traffic island. Go left along the quieter road signed for Westlands which follows the wall surrounding Westwood Park. In about half a mile, and at the end of the wall, you will pass the ornate entrance to the Westwood Estate.

This is the end of your first section and ahead of you is a T-junction at Boycott Bridge. If you wish to reach Droitwich centre just turn right at the T-junction and follow the road into the town.

2

DROITWICH to CHADDESLEY CORBETT

8½ miles

A few miles south of Kidderminster it fell dark and the unfortunate soldier who, because of his alleged local knowledge, had been appointed guide, found himself hopelessly lost.

MAPS: Landranger (1:50,000) 139 & 150; Pathfinder (1:25,000) 953 & 974.
PARKING: Public Car Parks in Droitwich or roadside near Boycott Bridge. Roadside in Chaddesley Corbett
TOURIST INFORMATION: Droitwich (01905 774312) Bromsgrove (01527 31809).
START: Boycott Bridge, Droitwich (GR 885634)
FINISH: 'The Swan' Chaddesley Corbett (GR 893737)

BETWEEN the entrance to the Westwood Estate and the Boycott Bridge T-junction there is a sign pointing left for Westwood. When adjacent to it go left through a gateway and immediately left again, left of allotments, to a gate. On the other side initially follow the edge of the allotments and then follow the path as it bears left through the trees. Cross a gated step stile and walk forward with the left hand iron fence until reaching a concrete estate road. Go over the road and continue forward on a long field crossing. *This path is well walked and usually easily identified. Should it have been recently ploughed however then the general heading is due west, 270 degrees.*

As you progress across the field you will see Great Pool to your left and the impressive Westwood House (now apartments) to the right. Built on the site of a former medieval Nunnery the house's former religious connections are remembered in the name of Nunnery Wood, which you will soon pass through.

In a while your cross field path will bring you to an unsurfaced farm track which you cross to continue your line until meeting a surfaced track. Cross this also, heading for the woodland ahead, but bearing a little more right (295 degrees) to meet and merge with a right hand fence near greenhouses. Continue forward with the fence to arrive at its pointed corner on the edge of the trees where you now meet the incoming 'Wychavon Way' – *note the 'W' waymarks.*

Turn acutely right with the waymarks to follow the fence (right) and tree edge (left). Soon this enclosed bridleway will bring you to a gate through which you walk across the sloping pasture to another gate a short distance in front. Through this maintain the same line to meet a gate in front of a small stone building. Go through the gate into Nunnery Wood and follow the clear track forward to soon exit the trees through a gate onto the edge of a sloping field.

Walk straight ahead up the centre of the slope(40 degrees) heading for the gap/gateway in the opposite hedge. Through this continue forward on a broad track heading for the industrial units in the distance. Arriving at the perimeter fence go left with the track to meet a road. Go right along

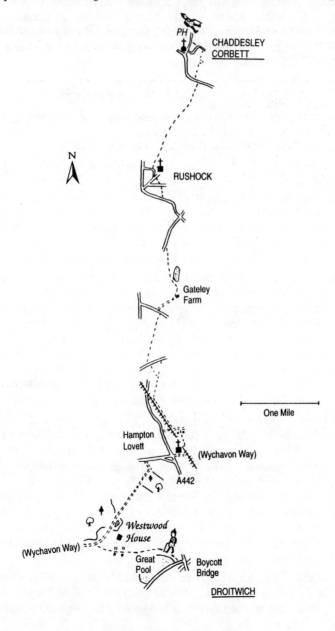

PH

CHADDESLEY CORBETT

N

RUSHOCK

Gateley Farm

One Mile

Hampton Lovett

(Wychavon Way)

A442

Westwood House

(Wychavon Way)

Great Pool

Boycott Bridge

DROITWICH

the road as far as the 30 mph signs where you turn left along a signed bridleway and 'no through road'. This brings you to the A442 in Hampton Lovett. Cross the road and follow the sign to the church.

Outside the church there are interesting memorials to the Doverdale family. It is said that Cromwell rested his horses here during the Battle of Worcester.

At the church leave the Wychavon Way by turning left through the lychgate and passing immediately left of the church down to a broken wicket gate. Walk through the tunnel under the railway to enter a field. In the field go half left (350 degrees) aiming just left of the right hand house. This line will bring you into a hedged green lane and so forward to a T-junction with a crossing farm road.

Go left along the farm road as far as the railway bridge. Do not cross it, instead go right to follow the railway fence and field edges.

The coppice that you can see on the other side of the railway is King's Wood!

Entering a third field leave the railway and go half right, diagonally across the field centre, aiming for a distant field corner (15 degrees) well right of the white gable end of a house. At the corner cross a footbridge into another field and then go half left (350 degrees) aiming for the left edge of a line of Leyland Cypress trees. This brings you to a step stile in the field corner immediately followed by a ditch bridge and another step stile. Over these go forward the few yards to cross a footbridge in front of the white house noted earlier. Now go left along the drive to meet a lane.

At the lane turn left for about 10 yards and then right through the first of two gates. Entering a field follow the left hedge to a step stile over which you immediately go through a fence gap into a nursery. Pass just left of a water tank and then go left and right to pass left of glasshouses. Beyond the glasshouses go a little right to a field corner and a stile next to two gates. Over the stile go left, through a gate, to follow the right hedge/fence of a narrow pasture. Now following a generally north-north-easterly line, passing through gates or over stiles and still with the right hand hedge/fence, reach a lane on the edge of Cutnall Green.

Go left for 15 yards and then right with the surfaced service road to reach a white house. At signs for Gateley Farm, The Homestead and Bryan's Green Farm, cross a cattle grid and follow the tarmac all the way to the wall surrounding 'Glynside Barn'. Here go through the gate signed 'Gateley Farm' to follow the wall forward. At the end of the tarmac, and just before the farmhouse, turn left along the edge of a pool and quickly right to follow the left hand hedge and a right hand line of trees. A few yards before the bottom corner – and just before the end of the line of trees – go left over a fence stile and so right to cross a culverted stream. Follow the clear track forward to enter a field.

In the field a large pool has been constructed and in front you will see its dam and outflow pipe. Swing left to cross the outflow (or the dam if that isn't practical) to then follow a hedge and the original stream (left) soon accompanied by a hedge on the right. Follow the narrow pasture to cross a step stile and so follow the left stream all the way to a small pool just before overhead power cables. Just past the pool there is a double fence stile in the left fence which you cross into another field. Here go forward towards the opposite corner where you cross another double stile immediately followed by a signed stile onto a road.

Turn right along the road, passing Beech Elm Farm, and follow it for about a third of a mile to a cross-roads. Here go left, signed Rushock and Cakebole, and follow this lane (Lunnon Lane) for a little short of half a mile to a point just before a black and white timbered house on the left. On the right there is a signed and gated fence stile which you cross into a field. Walk forward with the left edge for 75 yards to a gate. Go through the gate into the adjacent field and walk forward, cutting the right corner, heading due north. This quickly brings you to a stile in the opposite hedge and so onto a narrow lane. Cross the lane and the stile opposite and now go half left (330 degrees) aiming for the large white house. This takes you over a stile near the entrance to Court Farm. Do not go through the entrance to Court Farm but instead join the surfaced lane where you turn right and follow it to the church.

The church of St. Michael and All Angels, Rushock is a good place for a break. Placed on the edge of this tiny village it sits on a low escarpment and offers good views across North Worcestershire.

Behind the church is Court Farm which was once Rushock Court and the home of Roman Catholics. Catholic priests were often sheltered at the Court and during this time it is believed that one was beheaded here.

To continue your journey: immediately past the church the lane goes left and down the bank. On this bend a public footpath sign directs you right to a recessed and gated step stile. Cross the stile and walk forward with a hedgerow on your left. Your way quickly becomes enclosed on both sides and in a little while swings left and down to a gated step stile in a fence. Over this go right with the right hand hedge/fence to another stile in the corner. Crossing into another field go straight ahead, across the centre, aiming for a protruding hedge corner (30 degrees) opposite. At the corner maintain your line by following the left hedge to cross a gated stile into another field and then, still following the hedge, arrive at another stile in the next corner.

Over this you now have about three quarters of a mile crossing field centres, and a series of stiles, until reaching the A448 – your general bearing is north-north-east.

Crossing the last stile onto the A448 turn left for 80 yards and then right with the public footpath sign which takes you along the perimeter fence of a nursery. Beyond the nursery walk along the field edge with the brook and hedge on your right. This will bring you into a recessed, rectangular corner where you will meet a gate in front of a pool outflow. Do not go through the gate, instead continue following the hedge/fence to quickly reach the protruding corner. Turn right with the hedge/fence and in 75 yards meet a step stile, which you cross, to continue your line now with the hedge on your left. Soon arriving at a crossing track go left, now with hedges on both sides, to reach Vicarage Farm (a barn conversion) where the track becomes surfaced and swings left. Leave the track at the corner to cross a fence stile and go straight ahead with the line of power poles. Soon passing through green gates you will quickly emerge onto Chaddesley Corbett's main street opposite the Swan Inn.

Chaddesley Corbett has a wide mix of architectural building styles – from Tudor to present day – together with two pubs which between them provide probably (in my view anyway!) the best two real ale brews in the Midlands.

The striking parish church is the only one in the country dedicated to St. Cassian – it is believed the saint was murdered here!

3

CHADDESLEY CORBETT to HAGLEY

8 miles

So, still south of Kidderminster and finding themselves lost, the King's party held a 'council of war'. Amongst the party was a member of the Giffard family of Chillington Hall near Boscobel. A strong Roman Catholic family, they were Royalist supporters who, because of their religion, were well versed in subterfuge and the hiding of priests. Consequently it was decided that the king should make for Boscobel, firstly passing through Stourbridge.

For these and other reasons it is very difficult to ignore Harvington Hall, a well known moated manor house which is on your route. Harvington Hall was owned by another prominent Roman Catholic family, and today still contains many 'priest holes' and secret passageways. Consequently it was very much on the 'recusant priest circuit'; must have been well known to the Giffards and, therefore, considered loyal to the crown.

Though I have no hard evidence whatsoever to support the theory: the religious factor, plus the party's 'conference' location and destination, make me feel that Harvington Hall must have featured somewhere in the plan of action, if only as a contingency plan. At the very least their location and subsequent route must have taken them very close to the Hall.

MAPS: Landranger (1:50,000) 139; Pathfinder (1:25,000) 933 & 953
PARKING: Roadside in Chaddesley Corbett. Side-roads at Hagley.
ALONG THE WAY: Harvington Hall. Hagley Hall.
TOURIST INFORMATION: Kidderminster (not open all year) (01562 829400). Bromsgrove (01527 31809).
START: 'The Swan' Chaddesley Corbett (GR 893737)
FINISH: 'The Spencers Arms', A456, Hagley (GR 914810)

L EAVING Chaddesley Corbett, head north along the main street. Soon after crossing a stream bridge go left along the road signed for Stourbridge. In about 300 yards, and just before the top of the rise, you will meet 'Green Acres' on the left and the white 'Beauty Bank Cottage' on the right. Here go left on the tarmac to pass right of 'Green Acres' and so enter a green lane. Quickly arriving at a gated step stile do not cross over, instead, immediately in front, turn right through a hedge gap.

Entering a field walk forward across the centre to pass immediately right of a power pole. This line will bring you to a protruding hedge corner and the bend in a farm track. Here join the track and, maintaining your line, follow the hedge down to a gate in the next corner. Pass through the gate and follow the right hedge/fence for another 150 yards to meet a fence

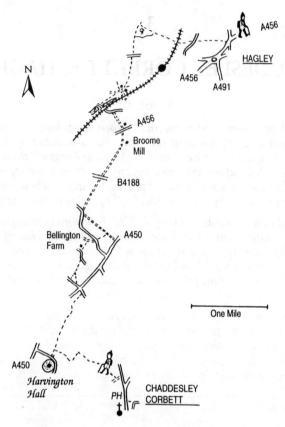

stile right. Cross over to continue your north-westerly direction with the hedge/fence now on your left. Following this line for some way will bring you to a crossing hedge with a farm track on the other side.

Go through the hedge gap in front and immediately turn left along the track which you follow to the next corner. Follow the track as it swings right, soon passing a path junction and a sign for Harvington Hall, and stay with it until reaching another crossing hedge where ahead you can see houses. Your track now goes through and turns left to quickly meet a surfaced lane. Follow the lane left to the moated Harvington Hall.

The Hall is open to the public but not at all times. Telephone 01562-777267 for details.

To continue on your way retrace your steps along the surfaced lane and on the bend go right along the track you left earlier. Following the right hedge do not go through the gap but continue heading north-north-east along the field edge and with the hedge on your right.

At the end of this very large field enter the next through a gap and maintain your line but now with the hedge/fence on your left. In about 400 yards, just before the next corner of this second field, you will come to a gap in the left hedge through which, just a few feet away, you will see

Harvington Hall

a stile in a fence. Go through the gap and over the stile into an 'L' shaped paddock. Now walking half left, and aiming just right of the large white house ahead, reach an inverted corner where two fence stiles take you into a short section of enclosed path. At the end of this cross the fence stile left and turn right to resume your original line with a right hand fence. This will soon bring you to a stile onto a lane.

Go left along the lane to reach the A450. Cross this main road to enter the lane opposite. In about 100 yards you will come to a break in the right hand fence (in the fullness of time this should have a stile and signpost) which you go through into a field. Walk diagonally left (340 degrees) across the field to reach a crossing path/track which is simply the boundary between two fields – to the right you can see the stranded end of a hedge. Here go right along the path/track to pass under power lines and meet the stranded hedge. Pass right of it to quickly meet a surfaced farm road at a bend.

Should this short section of diagonal field crossing be obstructed for any reason it is possible to continue along the lane for another 100 yards and turn right through a gateway into the field and forward along the path/track to pick up the line of the definitive route again and so pass under the power lines to meet the stranded hedge – see sketch map. This alternative should only be used if the definitive route is not negotiable.

Continue forward with the farm road – field edge left, hedge right – towards Bellington Farm where the road goes sharply left. Leave the tarmac on this bend and go right, through a gate, into a field and then immediately left to pass between the garden hedge left and tennis court right. At the end of the tennis court go through a gate into a sloping field and walk forward and down, aiming for the right edge of a ivy covered brick building. Here there is a stile in the fence corner which you cross onto a track. Go forward on the track to pass a second brick building and so rise to meet a narrow, surfaced lane. Cross this and walk to the fence a short distance ahead at the bottom of the slope. At the fence follow it right for 30 yards to a step stile. Crossing over go half right up the slope to meet a stile onto the ridge top track. On the track go left.

Here you have good views left across Worcestershire and right to the West Midlands.

Soon the track begins a descent and brings you down to a lane. Turn right and, as the tarmac goes left, leave it on the bend to continue forward and through a gate onto an enclosed bridleway. Descending, pass through a hunter's gate and then through a small woodland to enter a field corner. Here continue your line along the right edge of the field to then pass between houses to the B4188.

Cross the road to the signed bridleway opposite and follow the broad unsurfaced track. Soon, with field edges left and the woodland right, the bridleway takes you left of Broome Mill (a house) to join a drive and so up to the A456. Here go right and then left along the signed bridleway at the side of Harborough Farm.

To your left are the wooded slopes of Harborough Hill and, hidden by the trees, Harborough Hall which dates from the seventeenth century. The Hall was once the home of William Penn – founder of Pennsylvania in the USA.

As the tarmac swings left towards a house you go straight ahead with the right hedge to eventually meet a road at a bend and railway bridge. Go under the bridge and in about 60 yards, immediately before 'Stakenbridge Farm', go right over a stile to follow an enclosed path along the side of a large pool. This will bring you to Brakemill Farm.

Down to your right you will see the restored water wheel on the side of a converted mill.

Arriving in front of the farm buildings, and at the end of a surfaced road, go very slightly left to pass between a detached house left and barns right on an unsurfaced farm road. This brings you into a field where you continue forward with the right hand hedge. Passing through a gate your path becomes enclosed and soon joins a road.

You have now joined the North Worcestershire Path (NWP), a 21 mile, long distance regional footpath created by Hereford and Worcester County Council. Note the special waymark arrows for you now follow this route as far as Hagley, the end of this section.

Turn right on the road for 25 yards and left over the signed and gated stile. Follow the left hedge to the end of the field where your path now becomes enclosed and rises to meet a stile almost at the top of the slope. Cross it and go immediately right over another to follow the right fence as it gradually descends.

Ahead you can see the Clent Hills and the leaning obelisk on Wychbury Hill.

In a little while you will arrive at a double stile which you cross to continue the same line, now on the edge of a school playing field and with a left hand hedge/fence. This soon takes you across a railway bridge and onto the edge of a small housing estate.

Follow the estate road (Wynds Point) forward and up – there are NWP waymarks on lamp posts and telegraph poles – to reach its end at a small cul-de-sac. Here go forward on the tarmac footpath to swing right in front of houses with a stream and fields to your left. This path will bring you to Worcester Road which you cross to the gated step stile opposite.

Over the stile follow the initially enclosed path, with the stream to your left, to cross a series of NWP waymarked stiles and so reach the final enclosed section between houses and a telephone exchange. This brings you to the busy A456 at Hagley – across the road is The Spencers Arms.

Hagley Hall is just a short distance from The Spencers Arms.

Hagley Hall as it was

4

HAGLEY to STOURTON

(via Wordsley)

9 miles

At night, the Royal party passed through Stourbridge where they sought refreshment.

MAPS: Landranger (1:50,000) 139; Pathfinder (1:25,000) 933
PARKING: Side-roads at Hagley. Lay-by on A458 at Stewponey Lock, Stourton.
ALONG THE WAY: Hagley Hall. Wychbury Ring and Obelisk. Stourton Castle.
TOURIST INFORMATION: Kidderminster (not open all year) (01562 829400). Wolverhampton (01902 312051)
START: 'The Spencers Arms', A456, Hagley (GR 914810)
FINISH: Stourton Junction (Staffs & Worcs/Stourbridge canals) Stourton (GR 863851)

LEAVING The Spencers Arms at Hagley, head east-north-east along the A456 – signed Birmingham. In about 275 yards after the traffic lights you will come to Monument Lane, a signed no through road, on the left. Go left along it and follow it up to a turning area.

To the right is a concrete structure relating to the Elan Valley Water Pipeline – Birmingham's water supply!

Here go forward to a fence stile just right of a gate and left of the concrete structure. Over it follow the shallow valley upwards soon on a nice terraced path which soon brings you to the extreme right hand corner of woodland. Here leave the terraced path to go right a few feet up to a fence stile next to a gate. Over the stile continue upwards with the woodland boundary on your left and the obelisk up to your right.

This obelisk, a well known landmark from many parts of the West Midlands, is several degrees off the perpendicular and extremely dangerous – so keep well away. To the left, and in the trees, is Wychbury Ring hill fort, credited by some people as the site of a battle that took place between Britons and Romans. On this occasion the Britons won!

As you crest the slope you will come to a junction of paths and two fence stiles. Go left over the wider one and cross the narrow neck of the woodland to another fence stile a short distance in front. Crossing this takes you into an enclosed path. Quickly passing a right branch, follow the fenced path/track for about half a mile all the way down to the houses on Pedmore Lane.

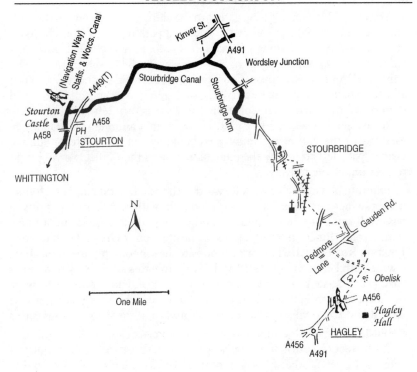

Here you are right on the edge of built-up Stourbridge and from here follows about 2½ miles of walking through residential areas, and then the town centre, to reach the Stourbridge Arm of the Stourbridge Canal.

Turn right along Pedmore Lane and follow it to pass a right junction (Pedmore Lane again) and continue up the same road, now named Gauden Road. In a little while go left along Sandhurst Avenue and in just a very few yards left along an enclosed tarmac path which soon emerges in a cul-de-sac- of bungalows. Walk forward, again for just a few yards, to then go right along another enclosed path between bungalows 8 and 9. This brings you down into a tree lined hollow and to a footbridge. Crossing the footbridge, following a railed path, and keeping on the right side of the stream will, in about half a mile, bring you to the A4036 (Ham Lane) adjacent to Old Ham Lane.

Go right along the main road, crossing it at the bollards, to continue right for another 15 yards where you turn left along a tarmac path into another cul-de-sac (Brockmoor Close) to then follow it down between houses to a T-junction. Here go left (Thicknall Drive) for just a few yards and then right along the concrete path between houses 4 and 6. This brings you into an open area with the re-emergent stream again on your left. Follow the path to s)on pass under a railway bridge and on the other side continue forward and up to the church (The Parish Church of St. Mary, Old Swinford) ahead.

Arriving at the metal kissing gate into the churchyard, do not go through but instead turn right to follow the enclosed path down to Church Road. Here walk down and along Church Road – *note the rambling, castle-like half timbered building on the right* – to meet the B4186 in front of 'The Labour in Vain' public house. Cross to follow the road opposite (Red Hill) and soon turn right along Red Hill Close (leading to Arlington Court) and then down into Arlington Court. In a few yards turn left along a tarmac path between houses 11 and 15 (no 13!) and enter another road. Continue forward to the end at the railway embankment in front. Here follow a tarmac path left to follow the embankment and then quickly swing right to pass under the railway.

Entering playing fields walk forward with the left hand fence and follow it as it swings left. In just a few yards go right with some concrete posts to pass well right of school buildings and so meet double gates and a single onto a road (Junction Road) almost opposite Coney Green. Go left along Junction Road and in a few yards (opposite the school sign) turn right along a wide path between houses 29 and 31. Follow this all the way to another road (a cul-de-sac) and turn left to follow it up to its end. Continue forward on another path between houses 25 and 44 which takes you right of a school and so down steps to continue forward at the back of houses to a road.

A few feet to your left is a railway bridge. Cross it and go immediately right along yet another enclosed footpath to swing left in 20 yards and so pass between the church and the fire station. This brings you to the ring road that encircles the very centre of Stourbridge like a medieval moat.

The safest way of crossing is to go left to the pedestrian crossing and then down and under the subway. On the other side go through Court Street – little more than a wide passageway – to join High Street opposite Barclays Bank.

Turn left to follow High Street and then Lower High Street as far as you can go. Here you come up against the other end of the Ring Road where you take the pedestrian subway at the side of The Woolpack Inn. After the first section of subway take the left hand section to then immediately go right up to a road sign indicating left 'Canal Street' and 'Old Wharf Road'. Join Amblecote Road and quickly turn left along the cobbled Canal Street to pass 'The Bonded Warehouse' – home of the Stourbridge Canal Trust – and then between factory buildings to join the Stourbridge Arm canal towpath. Follow the towpath forward and in about 1½ miles arrive, through a sandstone cutting, at Wordsley Junction.

It is known that the King took bread and beer at an inn near Stourbridge. Local tradition has it that the inn was actually in Wordsley and, though long disappeared, was on the site now occupied by a shop at the corner of Kinver Street and High Street. Though not really worth the detour (not even a plaque) it is only a short distance from Wordsley Junction and if you wish to make the journey then simply cross the roving bridge and go right (north east) along the Stourbridge Canal towpath. Leave the towpath at the first bridge (note the bottle kiln at the Glass Museum) and go left along High Street shortly arriving at Kinver Street on the left. At the time of writing the site was occupied by a fancy dress hire shop. To regain the canal simply follow Kinver Street to a public open space on the left. Cross the open space to meet the towpath and turn right.

If not making the detour then cross the roving bridge and head west (left) along the towpath of the Stourbridge Canal.

Very quickly you leave the industrial Midlands behind to enter a Staffordshire countryside where the canal-side scenery improves all the time. In a little over two miles a series of locks takes you under the A449 and forward to meet Stourton Junction. At the junction cross the bridge to the Staffs & Worcs Canal near to the large canal-side finger post – the end of this section.

On occasion I have come across mention of a Kinver Heath being on the King's route, though more authoritative accounts do not seem to mention it. Searching maps and enquiring locally has failed to identify this place. Although Whittington has been suggested to me as being the 'lost' Kinver Heath I have tended to discount this for reasons outlined in the introduction.

The very tenuous connection of a Kinver Street at Wordsley plus the facts that Kinver is only a mile from Stourton (as the crow flies); that Stourton is on a north-west/south-east line with Stourbridge; that as the King would have had to veer westerly after Stourbridge (so as to by-pass Wolverhampton but still head north for Boscobel) persuades me to a feeling, no more than intuitive, that Kinver Heath and the area between Wordsley and Stourton may be one and the same. In any event the Staffs & Worcs is a lovely canal to follow.

Ahead and across the River Stour you will see the unusual but historic Stourton Castle. Stewponey Lock and the A458 are but a couple of hundred yards south along the towpath. The Stewponey & Foley Arms, and bus routes, are within sight on the A449.

Should you wish to visit the Whittington Inn then go left (south) along the Staffs & Worcs for three miles and leave the canal by crossing left over the Whittington Horse Bridge to the Inn. Afterwards retrace your steps to Stourton Junction.

5

STOURTON to WOMBOURNE
(The Bratch)

7 miles

After Stourbridge, the King and his followers continued their journey to Boscobel.

MAPS: Landranger (1:50,000) 139; Pathfinder (1:25,000) 933 & 912.
PARKING: Lay-by on A458 at Stewponey Lock, Stourton. Car Park and Picnic Area at The Bratch, Wombourne (gates opened at 8 a.m. and locked at 9 p.m.).
ALONG THE WAY: Stourton Castle.
TOURIST INFORMATION: Wolverhampton (01902 312051).
START: Stourton Junction (Staffs & Worcs/ Stourbridge canals) Stourton (GR 863851).
FINISH: Bratch Bridge (Car Park and Picnic Area), Wombourne (GR 868938).

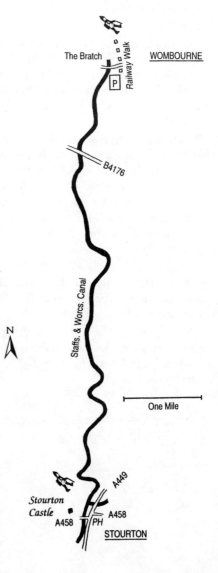

THIS *next section of the route could not be simpler to follow, or describe. Now you can put the maps away and enjoy this lovely canal built by James Brindley and opened in 1772. Joining with the Trent & Mersey Canal the system connects three of England's*

major rivers, the Severn, Trent and the Mersey. The route now coincides with 'The Navigation Way' as far as Bratch Locks.

From the finger-post follow the Staffs & Worcs Canal towpath north, signed for Wolverhampton, for the next seven miles until reaching Bratch Bridge – number 47 – the end of this section.

Leave the canal here to walk east along Bratch Lane for the car park and picnic area.

Before leaving the canal do have a look around the famous Bratch Locks which apart from the engineering content are, along with the octagonal toll-house, exceedingly picturesque.

6

WOMBOURNE to OAKEN

(with an optional diversion to Codsall for transport/services)

8½ miles.

Through the night the King continued heading north for Boscobel.

MAPS: Landranger (1:50,000) 139; Pathfinder (1:25,000) 912 & 891.
PARKING: Car Park and Picnic Area at The Bratch, Wombourne (Gates opened at 8 a.m. and locked at 9 p.m.). Roadside in Oaken. Public Car Parks, Codsall.
ALONG THE WAY: Wrottesley Hall.
TOURIST INFORMATION: Wolverhampton (01902 312051).
START: Bratch Bridge (Car Park and Picnic Area), Wombourne (GR 868938).
FINISH: Oaken (GR 857027) or Codsall railway station (GR 865033).

NOW *follows a stroll along the Kingswinford Railway Walk, an old Great Western Railway branch line which was one of Dr Beeching's victims in 1965. It was officially opened as a railway walk in 1981 and will take you to the outskirts of Wolverhampton from where you bypass the town to head north across country on your way to Boscobel.*

From The Bratch car park and picnic area, continue east along Bratch Lane to pass under the railway bridge. Turn immediately left up to the old railway station – *delicious cream teas available in summer* – and join the track bed to head north.

Follow the railway walk for two miles and then leave it by going left up steps immediately after the second 'under' bridge – number 40. Joining Langley Road go left to pass Market Lane and in another 75 yards go right through the narrowest of two hedge gaps at a public footpath sign. In the field walk forward with the left hedge, under power lines, to reach the next corner. Continue your line in the next field, but now with the hedge on your right, to reach a gate left of a large house.

Pass through the gate onto an unsurfaced lane and go left across the canal over Mops Farm Bridge. *To your left are the canal feeder reservoirs much patronised by local fishermen.* On the other side follow the farm lane forward, left of all the farm buildings, and stay with it as it swings right and left between barns to become a hedged and roughly surfaced lane. Follow the lane to its end at a tarmac lane.

Here go right and follow this lane as it swings left to a ford. Cross the footbridge and walk up to the A454. Over the main road take the signed bridle track opposite. This is quickly hedged on both sides and then just as quickly loses its left hedge. In another 400 yards or so, the left hedge re-appears at a point where your right hedge swings right. Follow the right hedge, always keeping it on your right, for almost three quarters of a mile to meet the right corner of Freehold Wood. Here turn right through a fence gap to join the farm track on the other side of the hedge. Go left along the track, right of the woodland, at the end of which you will meet

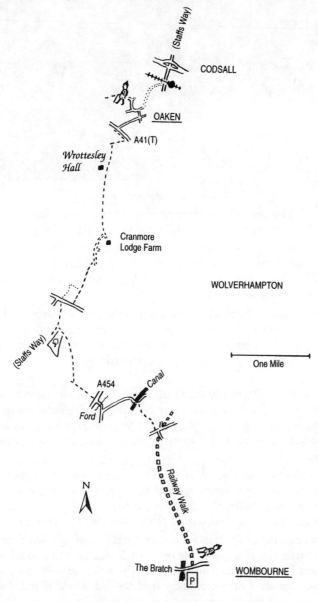

Wood Hall Farm and moat

a path/track junction and the Staffordshire Way – *which you now follow all the way to Oaken/Codsall.* At the junction bear right along the enclosed track and follow it all the way up Perton Ridge to meet a road.

Local legend has this sunken track as part of King Charles' route to Boscobel while at the same time it delights in the unusual name of Toad'snest (sic) Lane!

Turn right along the road and follow it for about 250 yards until almost opposite the gates to Far Park. Here go left through a hedge gap into a field and follow the right hand hedge forward to then cross a golf course, still with the remains of a hedge right, until arriving at its end and a hedge gap.

To avoid the 250 yards of road walking there is a short permissive route as follows. From Toad'snest Lane just cross the road to enter the field next to the Perton sign. Following the left hedge to a corner go right to soon meet the hedge gap mentioned at the end of the previous paragraph, here a left turn is required.

At the time of writing there is also a diversion application before Staffordshire County Council seeking to move the definitive line of the bridleway a short distance away from the house at Perton Orchard, so if using the definitive line look out for the possibility of diversion waymarks.

Go through the hedge gap for a centre field crossing on a clear route. This will bring you to a gap in the opposite hedge next to a stand of trees. In the next field continue forward, with the stand of trees on your left. *Ahead you can see Cranmore Lodge and the old World War II buildings which were built in 1941 to accommodate Dutch troops.* In a while the track swings right but you go straight ahead through a gap to follow an enclosed track which passes left of the buildings and reaches a gateway and a crossing track.

Turn left along the crossing track and follow it to another fence gap and so into a field. Follow the left hedge for half of its length when you will come to a gap where the bridleway goes left and across the centre of the adjacent field. You go left through the gap but then immediately right to follow the other side of the hedge to its end just in front of an old oak tree. *To your left you will see Wrottesley Hall.* Here go forward to pass the oak tree and then the left edge of a small stand of trees to cross a farm track and a field centre to another solitary tree and the opposite hedge/fence where there is a farm track. Join the farm track by going right – on the other side of the hedge/fence is the surfaced drive to the Hall – and following it for about 25 yards where you cross a stile onto the drive. Go right along the drive and follow it to a gated step stile at the edge of a golf course.

Over the stile swing immediately left to pass left of the wooden clubhouse where a grassy path follows garden fencing to a protruding corner and a power pole. Here continue forward on a well trodden path, through scrub woodland and following the edge of the golf course, to swing right and then finally left over a sleeper footbridge to enter the edge of a field.

In the field go right to follow the edge to the corner next to a house. Here go left to follow the wall – then hedge – that separates you from the busy A41. Soon you will come to a stile in the hedge that takes you down steps onto the A41.

Cross over to enter Shop Lane opposite and follow it all the way into Oaken. Arriving at a right bend go left along Oaken Lane which quickly brings you to a telephone kiosk, a Post Office letter box and the end of this section.

If you wish or need to divert to Codsall, whether for transport or supplies, then turn right at the telephone kiosk to follow the public footpath sign and pass a 'no through road' sign. Go through the gate at the side of Upper Lodge and follow the unsurfaced sunken lane that soon descends (offering good views to Cannock Chase in the distance) and, becoming surfaced, eventually meets a road opposite Codsall Railway Station. Turn left for shops and services.

7

OAKEN to BOSCOBEL

5½ miles

A detachment of Parliamentarian troops was stationed in Codsall. Arriving at Whiteladies (a house that no longer stands, but very close to Boscobel) both the King and his horse were taken inside the house!

MAPS: Landranger (1:50,000) 127; Pathfinder (1:25,000) 891.
PARKING: Public Car Parks in Codsall. Roadside in Oaken. Car Park at Boscobel House (please request permission).
ALONG THE WAY: Boscobel House.
TOURIST INFORMATION: Wolverhampton (01902 312051) and Telford (01952 291370) – Accommodation (01952 291723).
START: Oaken (GR 858029).
FINISH: Boscobel House (GR 836083).

T HE IMMEDIATE *area between Codsall and Boscobel has a meagre rights of way network; most of the little there is either doesn't lead anywhere or doesn't serve any particular purpose. Unfortunately, this means that the second half of this stage necessitates following a road. Although a minor road, it can be rather busy at times and whilst there is a grass verge for most of its length there are small sections where the verge is non-existent. For these reasons you may wish to omit this section and pick up the route again at Boscobel: as an alternative it is possible to take a taxi from Codsall to Boscobel (fare approximately £4 – 1994) – there is a bus, but it only runs once a week! If you decide to walk the whole section then please exercise care; and for you the route is now described.*

At the telephone kiosk in Oaken, continue along Oaken Lane to pass Middle Lane and stay with Oaken Lane to the end of the village.

If starting from Codsall then retrace your steps to the drive (opposite the Railway Station) that brought you from Oaken. Turn right and follow it to the entrance to Springfield House where the tarmac ends. Continue forward to follow the brick wall to its protruding corner where a public footpath sign points right to a kissing gate. Here you cease retracing your route by going right to enter a field and walk forward with the wall quickly followed by a fence. Leave the fence at its protruding corner to continue forward on a well trodden path and so reach another kissing gate into an unsurfaced lane. Turn left and follow it to the surfaced Oaken Lane where you turn right.

Passing the set back gates on the right leading to Manor House Farm, in about 100 yards the lane bends right. On the left of the bend is a gated

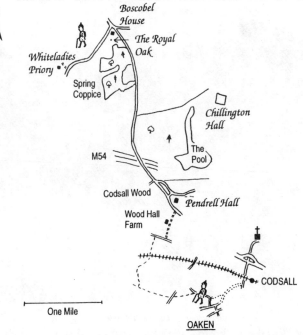

step stile which you cross into a field to walk forward with the left
hedge/fence. This brings you to another step stile back onto the road where
you cross to the unmade road opposite. Very quickly passing a picnic area
and through its parking space continue along the edge of the woodland as
the track becomes a rather muddy path and leads into the secluded Oaken
Lawn – a sort of long and narrow pasture. As you reach the house and
Oaken Lawn Riding School join the unmade road and follow it forward
for 100 yards to the footpath sign that points left and right.

Turn right to follow a woodland edge path. In a little while you will
come to a clearing on the left, with houses. Go left across the green to pass
immediately right of the right hand house (The Firs) and so enter trees
again on a clear path, quickly coming to a step stile. Crossing into a field
walk forward with the left hand hedge and ditch to meet two stiles in the
next corner. Climb the one in front to enter a second field and go half right
to the bridge at the far corner.

*This field is the flying headquarters of KARCS (Kinver Aeronauts Radio
Control Society) where you may witness one of their periodic meets.*

Cross the bridge over the railway and on the other side continue with
the track for a few yards to cross the left fence stile situated between two
gates. In the field walk half right to the far corner where a step stile takes
you into the corner of a second field. Here go immediately right for a few
feet to cross another step stile into a third field. In this field walk forward
and up with the right hand hedge/fence to a step stile onto a lane.

Go right along the lane and just beyond Husphins Farm turn left along
the surfaced lane which is also a signed public footpath. Follow this to pass

Boscobel House

right of Wood Hall Farm – *note the moat* – and so meet the road in front of Pendrell Hall.

Pendrell Hall is a Staffordshire County Council residential college and carries a name that has strong connections with this epic journey.

Turn left along the road to follow it for the short distance into Codsall Wood.

Codsall Wood is a small hamlet, with two pubs, standing on the edge of Chillington Park – ancestral home of the Giffards. Charles Giffard was of course a member of Charles' fugitive band and was leading them to Boscobel.

Suitably refreshed and fortified (but not too much!) now begin your walk along this fairly straight road – which crosses over the M54 – for the next two miles. This will bring you to a staggered cross-roads where a tourist sign directs you left for Boscobel House and the end of this stage.

Boscobel House is in the care of English Heritage and has extensive facilities, including a restaurant. Behind the house a path (not a right of way and only available if you have paid to enter the house) leads to the famous Royal Oak – a direct descendent of the original – where Charles hid on returning from his abortive attempt to cross the River Severn. It is intriguing to learn that a new export industry has grown around this tree – shipping 'royal' acorns to Japan!

The woodland, beyond the house and the tree, which you will have passed on the road, is Spring Coppice. It is recorded that Charles hid in a 'Spring Coppice'.

Boscobel gives nice views across Shropshire to The Wrekin.

8

BOSCOBEL to KEMBERTON

11 miles

Come the following evening the King and Richard Penderel left Whiteladies and, calling at Hubbal Grange for a meal, headed west for the River Severn. On the way they had a close encounter at Evelith Mill – disturbing the miller, they were forced to run for it.

MAPS: Landranger (1:50,000) 127; Pathfinder (1:25,000) 890 & 891.
PARKING: Boscobel House (please request permission). Roadside in Kemberton.
ALONG THE WAY: Boscobel House. Whiteladies Priory. Hubbal Grange. Little Nell's 'Grave', Tong. Evelith Mill.
TOURIST INFORMATION: Wolverhampton (01902 312051) and Telford (01952 291370) – Accommodation (01952 291723).
START: Boscobel House (GR 836083).
FINISH: Kemberton Church (GR 729045).

FROM Boscobel House head south-west along the lane and follow it for about three-quarters of a mile. On the right you will come to an unsurfaced track which is signed for Whiteladies Priory. Turn along it to pass right of the priory ruins and follow it to its end at a wooden hunters gate into a field.

Whiteladies Priory was an Augustinian nunnery founded in the twelfth century. Following the dissolution, the property was owned by a succession of Roman Catholic families and part was converted into a private house. It was here that Charles first arrived.

Entering the field walk forward and up with the right hedge/fence to meet a wooden wicket gate left of a field gate. Through the wicket gate

The remains of Whiteladies Priory

follow a right hedge to the buildings of Meashill Farm and then, through another gate, follow the waymarks through the buildings and so diagonally left across the stable yard to a gate. On the other side of the gate follow the tarmac lane away from the farmhouse and on a right bend leave the tarmac to go forward along a hedged green lane. *This lane now stretches for two miles all the way into Tong village.*

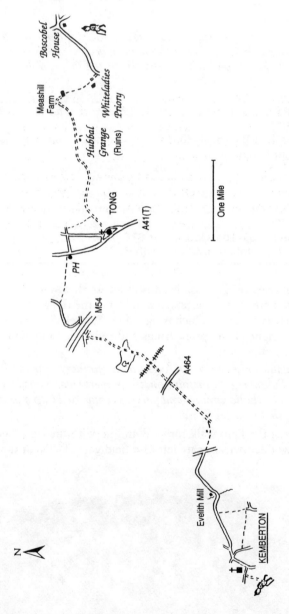

About half a mile along this green lane you will come to an area of scrub land on the left, Hubbal (Hobbal) Grange.

Today, all that remains of this timber framed building are two collapsed walls. Considering this was the home of Richard Penderel – who was so instrumental in effecting the King's escape and who shared so many of his dangers – and that Charles himself took a meal here, it is a disgrace that this historic building has been allowed to decay so rapidly and so recently.

Another mile along the green lane will bring you to Tong Hill Farm from where the lane becomes surfaced. About 200 yards past the farm, and just before houses, note the gated step stile on the right. Do not cross it yet but continue along the lane into Tong.

Having explored the village retrace your steps back along the lane to the step stile you noted earlier. Go left over it and forward with the right hedge, over a series of stiles, to arrive at a service road in front of houses. Follow it to a T-junction with a lane where you turn left. Go over a cross roads and follow the lane up to meet the A41(T) opposite the Bell Inn.

Turn right along this main road for just a few yards to the end of the filling station. Here go left through a wide hedge gap into a field where you follow the left edge and a wide farm track for half a mile. This takes you down into the attractive Pond Bay where, meeting a crossing track, you go right and left, between pools, to then rise up the sunken track to a lane.

Go left along the lane for half a mile to meet another road at a Y-junction. Turn right to pass under the M54 motorway where you will see another Y-junction on the left. Immediately past the 'Give Way' sign on the left go left through a gate to follow the hard-core farm road forward, through woodland and over a railway bridge, for almost 1½ miles to meet the A464. Cross over and take the unmade lane opposite when in

Evelith Mill

three-quarters of a mile you will come to a small stand of trees on the right and in front of a house on the left. Here leave the lane to go right on a path along the far edge of the woodland and quickly arrive at a wooden gate. Through the gate follow the fenced path along the left side of a house garden and so out to its drive where you continue forward and over the stile at the side of its gates. Continue along the farm track to meet a road opposite a junction.

Cross the road and take the lane opposite – signed Kemberton. Follow it for three-quarters of a mile descending to Evelith Mill and the Wesley Brook.

Beyond the brook continue up the lane for about 275 yards when, at the top of a rise, you will come to step stiles left and right. Cross the left one into a field and follow the left hedge/bank to its end where you will come to a step stile on the left. Do not cross it, instead strike right, up and across the centre of the sloping field (280 degrees) when after cresting you will see three houses at the far hedge. Following your line aim for the left edge of the right-hand house (white) and so join a lane through a gate gap.

Turn right along the lane and reaching a T-junction go left to follow this road through Kemberton to the church and the end of this stage.

It is difficult to imagine this quite rural backwater as it once was. In the days when water power was king the village possessed blast furnaces, nail making and a colliery. Today all of these are gone without trace and the village has reverted to its former residential/farming status.

A hasty departure from Evelith Mill!

9

KEMBERTON to NORTON

(via Madeley)

9 miles

Finding the River Severn heavily guarded the King and Richard Penderel sought refuge with Mr Francis Wolfe of Madeley who hid them in his barn. Abandoning the idea of escaping through Wales it was decided the King should return to Boscobel the following night.

MAPS: Landranger (1:50,000) 127; Pathfinder (1:25,000) 890.
PARKING: Roadside in Kemberton. Roadside in Norton.
ALONG THE WAY: The Royal Barn. Blists Hill Open Air Museum.
TOURIST INFORMATION: Telford (01952 291370) (Accommodation – 01952 291723) and Ironbridge (01952 432166).
START: Kemberton Church (GR 729045).
FINISH: A442, Norton (GR 726004).

FROM Kemberton Church follow the road south for a short distance to turn right into Hall Lane. At the cottage (WRS 1734) in front of the 'Masons Arms' pub turn left onto the unsurfaced farm road. Arriving at a cattle grid go diagonally right into a second field and then forward, diagonally, across the centre (215 degrees) to a stile right of the farthest corner.

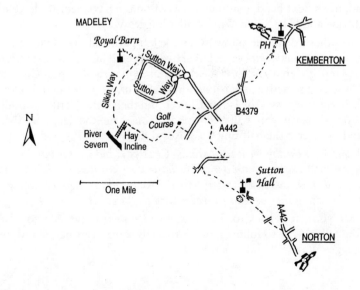

Over the stile, and on the same line, cut the corner of the next field to a hedge/fence gap. Cross the fence into another field (right of a fenced tractor way) and following the same line aim for the house and large barn ahead. This will bring you to the end of a stranded hedge in front of the farm. Here go right with the hedge to a stile onto a road.

On the road go left the short way to the Brockton fingerpost. Here turn right along the lane signed for Coalport which will bring you to the A442. At this main road cross over to the lane opposite and follow it until arriving at Brick Kiln Lane on the right. Turn right along the unsurfaced Brick Kiln Lane and at the last but one semi-detached house take the step stile on the left into a field. Here strike half right up the field to a step stile in the hedge.

In the next field your definitive line continues on the same bearing up to a point left of the woodland and right of a tree in another crossing hedge. Here it continues over this hedge and forward on the same line to the top right corner of the next field and so onto the public road – Sutton Way. However, at the time of writing, this second hedge and top corner was not negotiable, leaving you with no alternative but to take this following described diversion.

NB. At the time of writing, Shropshire County Council were carrying out footpath improvements in the area. The likelihood is that, when you walk this way, the definitive route will have been opened up!

Having crossed the second stile go left up the sloping field with the hedge on your left to pass through a gate and so to a second gate onto an unsurfaced lane. Here go right to meet the public road – Sutton Way.

At Sutton Way go right and follow it to 'Sutton Hill Roundabout'. Here go left, signed 'Local Centre', still on Sutton Way. Keeping on the right of the road, at its next bend, continue forward on the pavement to descend to a subway, and 'The Silkin Way', under Legges Way.

On the other side of the subway take the left path and then swing right with it, up to and between houses, to arrive at prefab bungalows – Station Terrace. Here go left and follow the road as it swings right to pass Cottage Farm Close and so arrive at a Y-junction near 'The Six Bells' pub. Follow Church Street as it passes the Parish Church and then follow it right, uphill. In a short distance you will see Upper House on the left and then immediately after it the half timbered 'Royal Barn'.

A plaque high on the barn wall states 'Charles II hid in this barn – 6th September 1651'. A large number of Parliamentary troops were billeted in Madeley and so it was in this barn that the King hid throughout the day. Later that evening they set out for the return to Boscobel.

Retrace your steps back to the subway and on the other side go right along the Silkin Way to follow it as it proceeds south-west parallel to the road, Legges Way.

The 'Royal' Barn, Madeley

The Silkin Way is a 14 mile urban walkway – named after Lord Silkin who was instrumental in the New Towns Act of 1946 – which connects many of the constituent towns which make up Telford New Town. You now follow it for a little over a mile as it passes by the Blists Hill Open Air Museum to the 'Hay Incline Plane' – an ingenious lift that was used to transport barges between the upper canal and the lower River Severn.

In only a short distance after the subway The Silkin Way rejoins the road and continues as a tarmac pavement alongside it. Soon passing the entrance to Blists Hill Open Air Museum you first of all pass under a footbridge and then a partially dismantled railway bridge.

Immediately after the second bridge The Silkin Way bears gradually left, away from the road, to pass through a short tunnel.

Just before the tunnel, and up to the left, you will see one of the Museum's exhibits – a beam engine.

In a little while the Way brings you to a bridge which carries the Hay Inclined Plane – signed 'Great Hay Incline'. Passing under the bridge your route now leaves The Silkin Way by taking the signed and stepped footpath on the left to follow the Incline Plane fence to the chimney stack and the remains of the engine house (being restored) at the top.

If time allows it is worth continuing along the Silkin Way for a few yards and then down steps on the right. Here there has been a lot of restoration work – which continues – and there is a pub, a tea room, a Tar Tunnel, a Tile Museum, the bottom canal and the River Severn. It is a veritable time capsule.

It is possible to continue even further along The Silkin Way (a further half-mile) to reach Coalport Bridge. On the other side of the river is a pub and a picnic area.

At the top of the incline, opposite the chimney stack, there is a gated step stile and finger post on the right. Cross over into a sloping field and walk forward and down to very quickly bear left up to a marker post near a fence around woodland. Go forward with the fence on your left and eventually come to another step stile which you cross into the woodland proper. Continue forward in the same direction, but now with the fence on your right, until reaching a bench seat.

Here you have a good viewpoint across the Severn Gorge. From this point a short section of the definitive route is tree covered and overgrown. The described route is the one in use at the time of writing.

From the bench seat continue with the fence for a little over 200 yards to a point where the fence begins a slight bend right and down. Here you will meet a rising, crossing path. Turn left and follow it up to a grassy crossing track. Now back on the definitive line, turn right along this track and follow it, first contouring and then gently rising, to the top of the woodland and the edge of a golf course. Continue forward on the track, which bears a little left, to quickly arrive at a wide crossing point over a culverted stream – on the other side is a pool.

Your way now lies directly across the golf course and is not waymarked. Do take great care to avoid flying golf balls!

Passing right of the pool, cross the golf course on a bearing of 85 degrees, to pass well left of a house, and so arrive at the protruding corner of a wooden fence – this is just behind a mound with conifer trees and close to the 15th tee. Go over the fence and turn left to follow the path between the fence and a right hand hedge. At the top of this enclosed path, just before Sutton Hill Farm, you will meet two step stiles – one in front and one right. Go over the right hand stile and walk forward along the edge of a field with the hedge on your left. This will bring you to another step stile onto a road.

At the road turn left and follow it all the way to Brick Kiln Lane – *the one you used earlier*. On the right, opposite the entrance to Brick Kiln Lane, is a gated step stile which you cross into woodland.

Following the left edge of the wood soon arrive at another step stile that takes you into a field. Continue your same direction, now with a hedge on your right, and at the next corner cross another stile and so continue with the right hedge to a gated step stile in the next corner. Crossing into the next field go left and up the sloping field with the hedge on your left. At the top corner cross yet another step stile and, keeping right of farm buildings, cross another (isolated) stile. Continue forward to a gate onto a roughly surfaced vehicle track.

Turn right along the track, passing a small house right and a large one left, where the track becomes a hedged green lane. Now follow this down – *with good views across the Severn valley again* – to meet a low breeze block construction on the left which stands in front of a bungalow. *There are several derelict cars and lorries hereabouts!* Immediately at the end of the low building go left to follow a path/track with a row of Leyland

Cypress left and a fence right. This will quickly bring you to a waymarked step stile into a field.

In the field follow the bottom edge and soon cross another step stile. On the other side go left to follow the left hedge up the sloping field. Arriving at a protruding corner go right, across the field, to a step stile in the fence – this is on a line just right of Sutton Maddock church tower. Over this now follow a direction aiming for the church tower which will bring you to a marker post on the edge of a crossing farm track. Over the track aim for, and walk to, the right hand corner of the churchyard wall.

St. Mary's parish church, and the adjacent Sutton Hall, are somewhat isolated from the scattered Sutton Maddock. Whilst the village dates from Saxon times the church is mostly Victorian, though the tower is of Tudor origin. Together with the accompanying pool it is an idyllic spot.

Passing between the wall and the pool follow the wall to a field corner adjacent to the lych-gate. Here you turn right to follow the left hedge just a few yards to a stile which takes you onto the tarmac service road. Go right for just a few feet and then right over a gated step stile into another field.

Following the right hand fence to the next corner go left just a short distance to cross a step stile into another field. Here go half left to pass well left of the nearest pylon to arrive at another step stile which is itself left of a gateway in the far left corner. Over this one now walk half right, on the same line, to pass under overhead power lines and so arrive at another stile, right of a gateway. This takes you onto a hedged farm road which you cross to the opposite stile and so into another field.

Cross the centre of this field, passing just right of the tree in the middle, to the stile opposite. In the next field go diagonally left across the middle to a stile onto the A442, next to a cottage. On the road go right into Norton – the start of your next stage.

Norton is an interesting village with a hundred house, an unusual school clock tower, village stocks and several thatched cottages.

Sutton Maddock Church and Hall

10

NORTON to BOSCOBEL

12 miles

Not wishing to risk Evelith Mill again, Charles decided to ford the river.

Arriving back at Boscobel in the small hours of the morning must have seemed the lowest point in the King's fortunes. He spent the following day in the famous oak tree.

> MAPS: Landranger (1:50,000) 127 and 138; Pathfinder (1:25,000) 890, 891 and 911.
> PARKING: Roadside in Norton. Boscobel House (please request permission).
> ALONG THE WAY: Aerospace Museum, Cosford. Hubbal Grange. Whiteladies Priory. Boscobel.
> TOURIST INFORMATION: Wolverhampton (01902 312051) and Telford (01952 291370) – Accommodation (01952 291723).
> START: Norton (GR 730006).
> FINISH: Boscobel House (GR 836083).

YOU *will recall that when you crossed Wesley Brook at Evelith Mill it was exactly that – a brook. The 'river' that the King recalled crossing was 'waist deep', which suggests to me that the crossing point was probably below the confluence of Wesley Brook and the River Worfe, possibly at Beckbury. This then is the way we are heading, though you have the benefit of a bridge to cross the river! As it happens, some five of these twelve miles are along country lanes which, fortunately, are fairly quiet.*

Leave Norton by following the A442 south – *fortunately there is a footpath alongside the road.* In about half a mile go left along the lane signed for Cotsbrook, Higford and Beckbury. Follow this narrow lane for almost a mile to meet the B4176. Here cross over and take the lane opposite, which is signed for Higford and Beckbury, and follow it for half a mile to a junction and a sharp left bend.

Go left with the bend (signed Beckbury) and in another 250 yards, at the bottom of a dip, go right through a gate gap to follow a clear track into trees. Now follow this attractive track through mixed woodland to then enter a field. Walk forward along the edge of this long field with the left hand hedge/fence until arriving at a corner. Here pass through a hunter's gate which is next to a field gate.

Continuing forward just a few feet will take you over a wide, grassy, crossing track. On the other side walk forward and then left down a bank to its base. At the bottom follow the bank forward to the new, large,

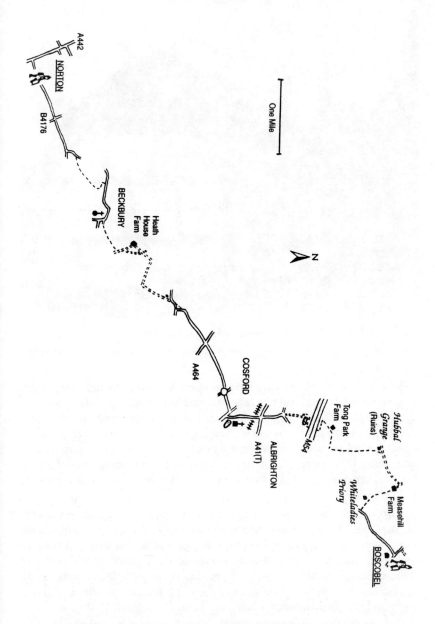

building within the Water Treatment Plant. Reaching the perimeter fence turn right and follow it to a hunter's gate onto a road.

Turning right now follow this road for half a mile all the way into Beckbury, and to its church.

On the way, and just before entering this attractive village, you will quickly cross the River Worfe, a tributary of the River Severn. Shortly after

The Hundred House, Norton

this you will pass 'The Severn Stars' pub which has a particularly attractive inn sign.

Stay with the road until just past the church where it swings sharp right. You go straight ahead along a lesser tarmac lane which quickly becomes a short, unsurfaced and hedged green lane before emptying into a field. Here you have a large field crossing so, bearing a little left (70 degrees), follow this line until adjacent with the bend in a track to your right. Here modify your line a little more left (60 degrees) to aim for the orange top of a pipe line marker post. After crossing a track this will bring you to a gap in the field corner.

Through the gap go left along a concrete farm track heading towards Heath House Farm. Just before the farm you will come to some bungalows. Here turn right to pass right of the bungalows and a large open barn. Swinging slightly left with the concrete meet a T-junction with another concrete track coming from the farm. Go right with this to pass Heath House Cottages (a large house) and follow it for almost a mile as it swings right and then left to reach a lane on a bend at Caynton Cottages.

Joining the lane go forward (right) to quickly arrive at a right bend. Here leave the lane on the left of the bend to go through a hedge gap near to a power pole. In the field go diagonally right (40 degrees) to the remains of the far right field corner where you exit the field, just left of a tree, into a lane just before a right bend. Go forward along the lane and round the bend to reach the A464.

Crossing the main road follow Bowling Green Lane, almost opposite, all the way into Albrighton.

Along this lane, first of all on the left, you will see the World War II hangers of Cosford Aerodrome and further over the more modern hangers and airstrip of the Cosford Aerospace Museum. Later, and on the right, you will see the disused, but lived in, windmill.

Arriving at a traffic island cross to take the continuation of Bowling Green Lane opposite, now through a residential area. Soon reaching a T-junction go right for a few yards and then left down Rectory Road. Quickly passing a pool, together with St. Cuthbert's Well and Jubilee Walk, arrive at the church. Continue with the road, past the church and then over a railway bridge, to meet the A41(T).

On the other side follow Shackerley Lane forward to arrive at a junction and bend. Leave Shackerley Lane to continue forward with the perimeter fence along Mill Lane. Beyond the married quarters the lane narrows to pass through gates and descend to the pool at Shackerley Mill. At the pool follow the drive left to the sluice gates at the pool dam. Immediately past the sluice gates go right up the step in the low wall to walk along the head of the pool to double gates on the other side. Turn right through the gates and follow the northern bank of the pool to another gate and so through the tunnel under the M54 motorway.

Despite the close proximity of the motorway the area around Shackerley Mill is very attractive.

On the other side of the motorway go through the hunter's gate next to the left hand of two gates. Take the concrete road forward, initially parallel to the motorway, and then follow it as it swings right to pass right of Tong Park Farm and its buildings. Immediately past the buildings go right through a gate and follow the fenced track down to enter a field. In the field go left and follow the left hedge/fence until reaching an enclosed pool. Here go through a gate and, still next to the pool, immediately right through a gateway into another field. Swinging left resume your northerly direction but now with a hedge on your left. At the next corner go through a gateway and forward with a left hand fence which will soon bring you to scrub trees, the ruins of Hubbal Grange, and the hedged and unsurfaced lane that you followed (Section 8) to Tong.

Now, just as King Charles did, it is simply a matter of retracing your steps to Boscobel House. Nonetheless the directions follow.

Accompanied by Colonel Carlis, the King hid in the Boscobel oak tree while Roundhead troops searched for him.

Turn right along the unsurfaced lane and follow it to its junction with a surfaced lane. Follow the tarmac right to Measehill Farm where, just in front of the farmhouse, you go left through the gate into the stable yard. Go diagonally right across the yard to the far right corner and follow the concrete path and waymarks through farm buildings to another gate into an orchard. Walk up the edge with the left hedgerow to a wicket gate into a field. In the field follow the left edge forward and down to a hunter's gate in the bottom left corner. Through the gate enter a hedged track and follow it, left of the priory ruins, all the way to a lane. Here turn left and follow the lane to Boscobel House.

11

BOSCOBEL to MOSELEY OLD HALL

11½ miles

At night, and escorted by the male members of the Penderel family, the King left Boscobel House for Moseley Old Hall by way of Pendeford Mill.

MAPS: Landranger (1;50,000) 127; Pathfinder (1:25,000) 891.
PARKING: Boscobel House (please request permission),
Moseley Old Hall (NT) (please request permission).
ALONG THE WAY: Boscobel House, Chillington Hall, Moseley
Old Hall.
TOURIST INFORMATION: Wolverhampton (01902 312051).
START: Boscobel House (GR 836083).
FINISH: Moseley Old Hall (GR 932044).

From Boscobel House follow the road north-east for a few yards to the T-junction. At the junction turn left (north) for about 300 yards until reaching a house on the right and a farm track for Pearse Hay Farm. Turn right and follow it to the farm. Passing a barn and the farm buildings the track swings sharp left in front of a gate. Here you leave it to go straight ahead, through the gate, and into a field.

Pearse Hay Farm, it is said, acquired its name during the time of the King's escape. Parliamentary troops were garrisoned at nearby Black Ladies Priory and they were used in the search for Charles. During their search they used pikes to pierce the hay ricks and this is supposed to have given the farm its name!

Entering the field follow the broad track that crosses it and pass between two pools to follow a right hand hedge to Eva Cottage and a narrow surfaced lane. Turn left along the lane – *to your right is the delightfully named Cream Pot Wood* – and follow it to then go right, signed Chillington, at houses. Passing 'Rose Cottage' and 'Hill Top' in about 400 yards pass a first green lane on the left. In another 300 yards you will come to a second unsurfaced lane, also on the left, signed for Hungary Hill Farm. Turn along this and follow it to the farm house. On the right and opposite the farm house there is a waymarked gate. Go through it and follow the edge of a pool for a few yards to the protruding corner of a hedge. At the corner go straight ahead down the middle of the field to a gated step stile in the opposite hedge/fence.

Entering a second field continue forward, a few yards parallel to the right hand hedge, to another gate. Go through this into a third field where you now go left to cross a culverted and fenced ditch. On the other side go right to aim for the step stile just right of the top left corner. Crossing this stile will take you into a hedged green lane. Turn left, passing a cottage, and so arrive at a track T-junction right of Chillington Farm. Here go right to meet a narrow tarmac road at houses.

Go left to follow the road which soon bends right to pass Horse Paddock Wood and the entrance to Chillington Hall. Just beyond the entrance pass a road on the left and in another 300 yards arrive at a hard-core surfaced lane on the left. Turn left, passing a couple of attractive thatched cottages, when, after the second cottage, the lane becomes a grassy (and sometimes muddy) track. Now follow the track all the way to a road – on the way you will cross the Staffordshire Way.

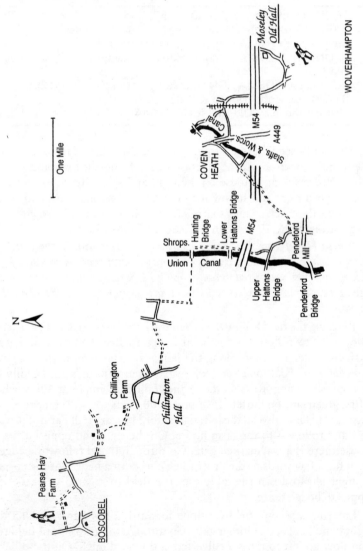

Estate cottage, Chillington

At the road cross over and follow the narrow lane opposite. In a little while, at a white house, the surfaced lane swings sharply left. *Ahead are views of Cannock Chase and the BT tower.* Here you go right along the unsurfaced lane/track to pass in front of a new bungalow. After a short enclosed section, the track passes under overhead power lines. Just a few yards beyond you will come to a bridleway sign in a hedge gap on the left. Go through the gap and follow the right hand hedge to a broad gap where you go through a gate to continue on the same line but now with the hedge/fence on your left. Follow this through two large fields to reach the 'Hunting Bridge' over the attractive Shropshire Union Canal.

On the other side of the bridge join the canal towpath and follow it south to pass under Lower Hattons Bridge, the M54 motorway, Upper Hattons Bridge and so arrive at Pendeford Bridge.

Just before Pendeford Bridge you will see woodland to the left and the tiny River Penk. These woodlands housed Pendeford Mill itself – which has long since disappeared – and Pendeford Hall – which has been demolished. The area is now a Nature Reserve.

At Pendeford Bridge leave the canal and go left (east) along Pendeford Mill Lane until reaching Pendeford Hall Lane where you turn left. Arriving opposite the entrance to Allen's 'Pendeford Hall' residential caravan park go right along a hedged green lane.

The Nature Reserve is a little further along Pendeford Hall Lane with a left turn to the entrance.

Now follows just over a mile of pleasant green lane walking, almost into Coven Heath. A few yards into this bridleway it becomes rather wet and muddy for the next 100 yards or so. However there is a readily apparent alternative which skirts left of the lane and rejoins it a little further on.

Following the green lane over the farm bridge that crosses the motorway will bring you to Shawhall Lane at a bend, next to a Water Treatment Plant. Go right to quickly reach Coven Heath Bridge (No. 69) which crosses the Staffordshire and Worcestershire Canal. Descend to the towpath and go left (north) to the next bridge which is (No. 70) Brinsford Bridge.

Leave the canal here to join the A449(T) dual carriageway. Taking great care at this very busy road, cross to the other side and go right (south) on the pavement.

The nearby Grange Farm in Coven is yet another of those places where Charles II is reputed to have stayed on his way to Moseley Old Hall, though there is little evidence to support this reputation.

Though a little longer it is possible to avoid the busy A449(T) by continuing further along the canal to (No. 71) Cross Green bridge. Pass under this bridge and leave the towpath through a hedge gap. On a lane go left to a junction, left across the bridge, and first right along Dark Lane. Follow Dark Lane for about half a mile to a T-junction at a railway bridge. Go left under the railway bridge and follow the directions from ➲ below.

Shortly arriving at Brinsford Lane (signed Moseley Old Hall) turn left. Now follows just over a mile along this road which fortunately has a pavement, or grass verge, for its whole length. Passing under a railway bridge Brinsford Lane now becomes the unusually named Cat and Kittens Lane.

➲ Stay with the road as it passes under the M54 and then by the 'National Grid Headquarters' to arrive at Greenfield Lane on the right. Do not turn, instead continue forward to quickly turn left along Moseley Road (again signed Moseley Old Hall) and follow this narrow lane to the next left turn.

It should be noted that, within close proximity to each other, there is a Moseley Hall and a Moseley Old Hall – the latter is your objective.

Here go left along this signed 'No through road' (Moseley Old Hall Lane) to arrive at the Hall itself.

12

MOSELEY OLD HALL to (the site of) BENTLEY HALL

9 miles

On horseback and escorted by Colonel Lane, the King made the short journey to Bentley Hall where Jane Lane had a permit allowing her to travel to Abbots Leigh, near Bristol – a major port!.

MAPS: Landranger (1:50,000) 139; Pathfinder (1:25,000) 891 & 912.
PARKING: Moseley Old Hall (limited – please request permission). Northycote Farm Country Park (car park closes at dusk). Roadside at Bentley.
ALONG THE WAY: Moseley Old Hall. Northycote Farm Country Park. Site of Bentley Hall.
TOURIST INFORMATION: Wolverhampton (01902 312051).
START: Moseley Old Hall (GR 932044).
FINISH: Site of Bentley Hall (GR 986990).

LEAVING Moseley Old Hall retrace your steps to the T-junction with Moseley Road. Here turn right and then just past the entrance to Moseley Hall, take the hedged track on the left which is a signed

Moseley Old Hall

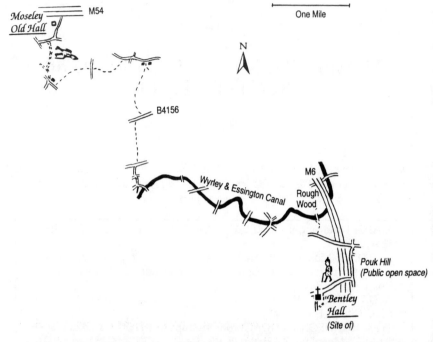

bridleway. Follow this for about a third of a mile to a T-junction with a crossing, surfaced bridleway – a former road.

These two bridleways, plus the following footpath, are public rights of way which are not shown as such on most Ordnance Survey maps.

At this second bridleway go left and follow it through vehicle barriers to its end, on a bend, next to Northycote Farm.

This part timbered farmhouse is 400 years old and now owned by Wolverhampton MBC who have incorporated it within the newly created Northycote Farm Country Park. According to the leaflet produced by the MBC, during his flight from Worcester, Charles II was declined shelter here. Can this really be so? – after all Moseley Old Hall is only a mile away!

The park covers an extensive area with many waymarked riding and walking routes; the farmyard has several types of livestock on display. Also boasting a Tea Room it is worth lingering if time allows.

Turn left along Underhill Lane and, just after the farm and before the car park, go left through a kissing gate along a signed public footpath. Keeping a hedge on your left follow it forward and then down to a footbridge over a stream. On the other side follow a hedged green lane up to a road.

Cross directly over the road to follow the signed footpath between houses 99 and 101. Quickly crossing a step stile continue forward to pass under overhead power lines and so enter a fenced path that descends between a sand quarry left and reclaimed land right. Rising, the path brings you to another step stile that takes you out of the quarry area and into another hedged green lane.

Joining a road go right and follow it for about a quarter of a mile to reach Manor Farm at the top of a rise. Here a public footpath sign directs you right to pass between the farmhouse and barns and so out to a cluster of gates. Here continue forward for the necessary few yards to pass immediately right of a tree and so follow a clear path between a left-hand hedge and the right-hand embankment that surrounds another sand quarry. Soon leaving the quarry behind, continue forward with the left hedge/fence for some distance before reaching a step stile. Cross over and go up the small embankment onto the track of a former railway bed. Go left along the track and so reach the B4156.

Here ignore the continuation of the old railway opposite and instead turn right along the B4156. In a short distance you will come to a road warning sign indicating a left bend. Just a few feet beyond the sign go left over a step stile into an enclosed footpath. Follow the footpath forward as it heads for the edge of the Midland conurbation.

In the far distance, on a clear day, you can see the radio masts on the top of the Rowley Hills. These hills sit in the heart of the Black Country – no longer black following the devastation of successive recessions! – and formed a natural barrier to the canal navigators of the last century. As a result the famous Netherton Canal Tunnel was engineered beneath them. This tunnel is on the next section of your journey!

In a while your enclosed path will bring you to a step stile onto a crossing track. Here you do a rapid right and left to resume your line along another fenced path. This will shortly bring you to a stile onto Linthouse Lane.

Here you are at the northern edge of the West Midlands conurbation. As the crow flies it is a tarmac covered twelve miles to the southern edge and open countryside again. However in the Midlands we have a unique network of canals, those latter day transport arteries that were not around in Charles' day. Now, to avoid the monotony of road and street walking, you are able to follow a unique route along the Midland towpaths; a time warp that transports you into the less hurried world of our more recent ancestors. Indeed I am constantly surprised how closely the canals follow the route taken by the King!

Cross Linthouse Lane and follow Ridge Lane opposite. At its end and T-junction with Moathouse Lane go left and then bear right along Moathouse Lane West to a canal bridge. Cross the bridge and turn right down to the towpath and pass under the bridge to follow the canal in an easterly direction. Now follows a canal walk of some three miles.

This waterway is the Wyrley and Essington Canal. Completed in 1797 it is a relatively early canal which has no locks and so has to meander along a contour route. It was this feature that earned the canal its affectionate nickname – The Curly Wyrley!

After a little over two miles, pass under Lane Head Bridge then under another bridge – a wide footbridge with the unusual name of 'Adam and

Eve' bridge – to then pass between Rough Wood on the opposite bank and landscaped reclaimed land on the right. At the next bridge – Bentley Wharf bridge – leave the canal by going right on a made, gravel path across the reclaimed land and soon reach a road opposite a school.

On the road, Bentley Lane, turn left and follow it all the way over the M6 motorway to a T-junction in front of the 'Magic Lantern' pub. Here turn right to follow Bloxwich Lane for half a mile as it proceeds parallel with the motorway.

At certain times of the day you may well find yourself walking faster than the motorway traffic moves! This is a particularly notorious bottle-neck section of the M6. To your left you will pass Pouk Hill Public Open Space, a former quarry now in-filled and landscaped.

Arriving at the next right turn, Churchill Road, follow it to re-cross the motorway. A short distance ahead and slightly left you will see the square tower of a modern church – this is your objective. Continue with Churchill Road, gradually leaving the frenetic noise of the motorway behind, until arriving at a zebra crossing just before the 'Old Hall' pub. Here go left between the 'Over 60's Centre' and the 'Family Centre' and up the bank to circular iron railings behind the church – the end of this section.

The last mile or so has not been particularly attractive, yet necessary, to reach this point – the site of Bentley Hall. A plaque within the iron railings informs you:

This cairn marks the site of Bentley Hall the seat of the Lane family from the fifteenth to the eighteenth century. September 9th 1651 King Charles II was sheltered here after the Battle of Worcester and disguised as a groom rode away at dawn next day to Long Marston via Bromsgrove with Mistress Jane Lane. October 20th 1743 the Reverend John Wesley persecuted by a mob was brought here from Wednesbury to appear before Mr Lane, JP. The site of this memorial was enclosed AD1934 and given by Mr S Chambers to the County Borough of Walsall. The cairn is composed of stones etc. from the old hall which collapsed in 1929 as a result of coal mining. The basaltic column on the top is from the adjacent Powke (*sic*) Hill quarry. This memorial was erected by the Walsall Historical Association and the deed of conveyance was handed by Mr D Parry JP. to Councillor S E Edge, mayor of Walsall this 29th day of May 1934.

Winifred E Knight – President

Hy Hartop – Hon Secretary

The site of the Hall is quite prominent with a commanding position over the surrounding areas. Today the views are radically different from those of 1651.

13

BENTLEY HALL (site of) to HALESOWEN ABBEY

16 miles

On horseback and with Jane Lane riding pillion, the King (disguised as a servant) and his party left Bentley Hall for Stratford-upon-Avon – a staging post on the route to Bristol.

MAPS: Landranger (1:50,000) 139; Pathfinder (1:25,000) 912 & 933.
PARKING: Roadside at Bentley. Leasowes Park, Halesowen.
ALONG THE WAY: Site of Bentley Hall, Netherton Tunnel, Black Country Museum. Halesowen Abbey and Fish Ponds.
TOURIST INFORMATION: Wolverhampton (01902 312051) Dudley (01384 250333).
START: Site of Bentley Hall (GR 986990).
FINISH: Halesowen Abbey/A456 by-pass (GR 976833).

AVING *made the pilgrimage to Bentley you will be anxious to regain the relative tranquillity of the canals. This next section is a particularly long one but has the advantage of taking you straight through the conurbation and back into rural countryside in one go.*

The highlight of this section has to be the Netherton Tunnel. The tunnel is unlit and, due to percolating water, the towpaths are wet. Consequently a waterproof jacket, stout footwear and a good torch with spare batteries, is essential. For those who may feel apprehensive or claustrophobic about it, a suitable alternative is described. The student of industrial archaeology will find much of interest throughout this section.

From the cairn continue forward to pass the rear of the church on a flagstone pavement. Quickly join a narrow tarmac service road (Cairn Drive) and go right to follow it to Queen Elizabeth Avenue. Here go left and follow the road all the way to the traffic lights on the A454 (Wolverhampton Road West). Cross this busy main road to the 'Lane Arms' pub in front of which you go left for a short distance to Bentley Mill Way.

Turning right follow Bentley Mill Way as it passes over the new Black Country Relief Road, through a small industrial estate and over the abandoned Anson canal arm. A few other new developments follow until the road brings you to the old aqueduct which carries the Walsall Canal over Bentley Mill Way. Go under the aqueduct and then right up a path onto the canal towpath.

The Walsall Canal was completed in 1799 and, despite successive recessions, there is still some industry along this waterway which give a glimpse of what the Midland canals must have looked like in their heyday.

Follow the towpath forward (west) for 4½ miles so passing through the heart of the Black Country to eventually meet, and pass, the Tame Valley Canal Junction. Continue forward with the Walsall Canal to meet your first locks at Great Bridge. At the top of the flight you will pass Ryders Green Junction to then arrive at Pudding Green Junction.

Here you go right to follow the Birmingham Main Line canal which has a towpath on both sides. Immediately cross over the first bridge (Albion Bridge) to gain the opposite towpath and continue in the same (north west) direction. Passing under two bridges will bring you to the Albion Junction where you go left (south) along the Gower Branch to pass locks and so reach Brades Hall Junction and the Wolverhampton Level canal. Here go right (north west) with the sign for Wolverhampton.

* If you intend omitting the Netherton Tunnel then leave the canal at the first bridge on the Wolverhampton Level (See p. 55).*

Staying with the Wolverhampton Level for another 1¼ miles will bring you onto the aqueduct over the Netherton Tunnel Branch – to the left, and below, you will see the tunnel portal. Descend either side of the aqueduct to follow either towpath to the tunnel entrance.

The Netherton Tunnel was opened in 1858 and was the last canal tunnel to be built in Britain. At 1¾ miles in length, and passing through limestone

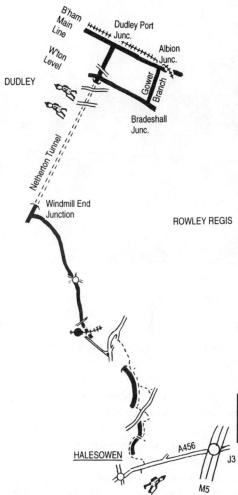

country, it is perfectly straight and will take the best part of three-quarters of an hour to walk through. Considering the relatively short passage of time since its construction it is surprising how the stalactites and limestone curtaining has formed to quite a remarkable thickness.

The canal emerges from the tunnel into Warrens Hall Park, a pleasant area of landscaped former colliery workings. Continue forward for the short distance to the Windmill End Junction where you go left along the Dudley No 2 Canal, signed for Hawne Basin – the limit of navigation on this canal.

Before making this turn though, a short diversion ahead to The Dry Dock, a theme pub with a canal boat for a bar, is worth the effort.

⊃ *Rejoin the Monarch's Way here if you have taken the alternative to the tunnel.*

Following the Dudley No 2 Canal for almost two miles will bring you to Gorsty Hill Bridge. This is immediately before the entrance to the Gorsty Hill Tunnel which has no towpath. So leaving the towpath at the bridge continue forward along and up the adjacent road – Station Road.

As you climb up over Gorsty Hill, note the incongruous ventilation shaft in the front garden of number 171.

Just beyond the crest of Station Road take the left fork to the T-junction with Coombes Road/Gorsty Hill Road. Go left and up Gorsty Hill Road to pass the Bell and Bear Inn and then Hillside Avenue. A little further on take a right turn, between houses 33 and 31c, along the approach road to the former British Steel works. Immediately past St. Ambrose church and in front of the works entrance, go left along the signed public footpath which follows the works perimeter fence.

Entrance portal, Netherton Tunnel

Follow the fence as it swings right, soon crossing heathland, to a protruding corner. Here continue right with the fence to quickly meet an inverted corner where you now follow the fence left and down.

Ahead and below you will see the emergent canal. Only a couple of factory chimneys now remain between you, the Clent Hills, and the promise of green fields heralding the end of the Black Country conurbation.

Arriving at the canal go forward with it to an iron footbridge. Here go left and up a path to cross an unsurfaced track over which you then cross a step stile into an enclosed path. Continue up, ignoring a stile left, to cross two more stiles and so join a crossing green lane. Here go right to cross a gated step stile and so meet the steep, dual carriageway, Mucklow Hill.

Cross over the road to go right and down to meet 'Sylvan Green' where a public footpath sign directs you left to Leasowes Park. Go left with the sign and past the houses enter a hedged green lane and so arrive at the park edge near two houses. Here go right on a tarmac park road to pass the car park and so reach the side of the abandoned canal.

Turn left to follow the canal and, using either of two available crossing points, change to the opposite bank. The canal is rapidly silting up and after the second crossing point (a footbridge) it is stopped off and trees have been planted. The 'towpath' continues forward to join a crossing surfaced path when, in just a few yards, you bear right through vehicle barrier posts to follow another surfaced path. Passing a children's small play area the path brings you to the busy A456 dual carriageway – the southern perimeter of the conurbation and the start of rural Worcestershire.

You have now completed the traverse of the mighty West Midlands conurbation in one go – well done! Across the dual carriageway are the lands of Halesowen Abbey, the start of your next section through entirely different surroundings.

NETHERTON TUNNEL ALTERNATIVE

This alternative will take you over the Rowley Hills, avoiding the section through the Netherton Tunnel.

Leave the canal at the bridge immediately after Brades Hall Junction (though you may like to first continue along the canal to view the entrance to the Netherton Tunnel, then return to this point). Go right to cross the canal and walk south along Lower City Road. Cross the A4123 at the pedestrian crossing and walk up City Road. (Or take the 120 WMT bus from the A4123 and alight at The Wheatsheaf.)

At the top of the hill (about three-quarters of a mile) you will meet The Wheatsheaf public house: turn right here along Oakham Road for about 50 yards. At the 120 bus stop on the left, turn left onto the path leading onto the golf course. Go forward (watching out for flying golf balls!) until you pass a black and white marker post on your right. Now swing right and drop down the hill to meet a stile beside a holly tree and behind which you will see the low roofs of Warrens Hall Farm Riding Stables. Cross the stile and turn left along the old quarry road.

Where the road becomes unsurfaced take the path branching off right and go down the hill towards a pool. Meeting a track follow this left to pass the pool, with a hedge on your right. Look out on the other side of the hedge for one of the ventilation shafts to the Netherton Tunnel.

The track soon descends between hedges to meet the B4171 at a public footpath sign. Cross the road and turn left to follow the B4171. You will soon pass another ventilation shaft on your right in Warrens Hall Park. Just past this go right into the park along a driveway and, reaching a group of trees, go right to a pool and walk left alongside it. After crossing the stream which exits from the pool go left towards the tall chimney of Cobb's Engine House.

Your path will take you behind the Engine House to meet a bridge ahead. Turn left in front of the bridge along the track with the canal below you on the right (though you may like to first go onto the bridge to view the end of the Netherton Tunnel). After a few yards you will see a 'Toll End Works' bridge on the right: go down towards this and onto the towpath where you rejoin the Monarch's Way (➲ on p. 53) or, if you are in need of refreshment, continue straight ahead to meet the Dry Dock public house.

14

HALESOWEN ABBEY to BROMSGROVE

13 miles

Near Bromsgrove the King's horse lost a shoe. Here Charles was obliged to play the anti-Royalist role, for the smith was a Parliamentarian supporter!

> MAPS: Landranger (1:50,000) 139; Pathfinder (1:25,000) 933 & 953.
> PARKING: Leasowes Park, Halesowen. Waseley Hills Country Park. Public car parks in Bromsgrove.
> ALONG THE WAY: Halesowen Abbey and Fish Ponds. Waseley Hills Country Park.
> TOURIST INFORMATION: Dudley (01384 250333) Bromsgrove (01527 31809).
> START: Halesowen Abbey/A456 by-pass (GR 976833).
> FINISH: Bromsgrove – Ye Olde Black Cross (GR 957704).

HAVING *covered the Black Country in virtually one go, you are now about to start a truly delightful walk through attractive, rolling countryside.*

Carefully cross the A456 dual carriageway to go right for about 100 yards down to a step stile and information board. Here go left over the stile and forward with the left hand hedge to its protruding corner and a step stile.

Ahead you can see the remains of Halesowen Abbey – there is no public access to the ruins but there are occasional open days. Soon you will pass through the embankments that formed the fish ponds. Though now dry the ponds are still clearly identifiable and in medieval times were used to breed fish, an important source of fresh food.

Over this second stile go forward (very slightly left) and through one of the embankments to cross a footbridge and so gain the opposite fence. At the fence go left to quickly meet a step stile at the junction of the fence and a hedge. Go right over the stile and cross the field, just right of a tree, to meet another step stile near a protruding corner in the opposite hedge. Crossing the stile continue forward, now with a left hedge, to merge with a farm track. Maintaining your forward direction quickly ignore and pass a stile in the left fence to now swing right and so cross a stream bridge. On the other side walk up to the opposite hedge/fence and arriving there go left, keeping it on your right. Quickly arriving at a protruding corner continue forward to cut the inverted corner and so rejoin the hedge/fence. In about 150 yards, and now terraced, your track will bring you to a gate where there is a step stile in the hedge.

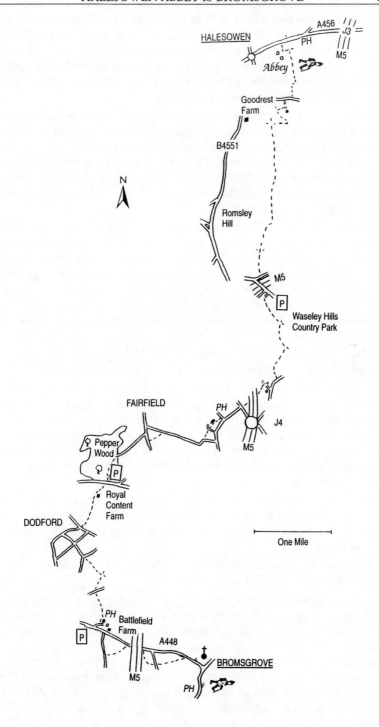

Cross the stile into a sloping field where there is a divergence of paths – one left and one straight ahead. Ignoring the left path walk forward across the centre to the brow. *Ahead you have good views of the two Clent Hills.* On the brow, and at a marker post, go left to meet the end of a stranded hedge which you now follow to keep it on your left. This will bring you to a field corner and a step stile onto a road.

On the road go right and follow it for about 300 yards where, just before the road descends a sunken section, you go left through a gate to follow a farm road. Just before the first of the farm buildings go right over a stile into a sloping field and follow the clear track down to an isolated stile just before a stream in the bottom of a shallow valley. Turn left 'over' the stile to walk upstream to a stile and footbridge in the hedge ahead, a short distance up from the stream.

On the other side walk up, left of a gully, to a marker post. Here go half left, to cut the field corner, and so arrive at the protruding corner of a hedge above another gully. *At the time of writing this protruding corner was effectively waymarked with a yellow dustbin lid!* Here continue forward above the gully to cut another corner and so reach another marker post. Here you will see a brick footbridge in the gully – descend to it. Crossing the bridge and a step stile go left, then right and left again up a stepped bank to emerge at a wooden shed and a crossing, unsurfaced road.

This is the edge of the Worcester Gun Club shoot and though there are several look-out points proceed with care if firing is in progress.

Turn right to follow the unsurfaced road down and across a bridged stream. Walk up the other side to a gated step stile over which you continue forward with a right fence to the corner of the pasture where a step stile awaits you. Crossing this now puts you into a field on the protruding corner of a hedge. Here go left the few yards with the hedge to the inverted corner of the field where there is a fence stile. Climbing over it continue forward with the left hedge.

To your right and across the field you will see a farm. Local legend has it that Charles called here for refreshment before continuing to Bromsgrove. As a result, it is said, the farm was renamed Goodrest Farm by which it is known today.

Your way now follows a fairly straight line south, for two miles, all the way to the Waseley Hills Country Park.

Staying with the hedge cross two more fence stiles and then quickly arriving at its protruding corner continue forward down to a footbridge. Over this maintain your line by crossing the next field centre to a step stile and finger post in a fence. Cross into the next field – *you have now joined the Illey Way whose special waymarks you follow to the Waseley Hills* – and continue your same direction for a long field crossing to its furthest side. Here you will meet marker and finger posts on the field edge which direct you down a made path to a footbridge at the bottom of Dowery Dell.

The path to Dowery Dell

Dowery Dell, a deep valley, was once spanned by a railway viaduct. Supported by two brick abutments and eight cast iron trestles it crossed 100 feet above the valley bottom and spanned 660 feet. Today, all that can be seen of this impressive piece of engineering is the occasional overgrown, blue brick, trestle base. The line and viaduct was dismantled in 1965.

Over the footbridge and up the other side go right along a made track through the trees. This will bring you to a step stile into a field. In the field go forward with the right hand fence, above the valley, and follow it for some way until meeting a step stile which takes you onto the other side of the fence. Here continue forward for the short distance to a crossing track.

Go over to continue forward on a broad track with a hedge/fence left and trees, plus the stream, right. In a short distance your track does a right and left kink to take you over the steam and forward through the trees. Rising gently the track then makes a final right swing to a gated step stile into a field.

Do not be tempted along the attractive grassy path that leaves the track just before the gated step stile. Though it continues forward through the trees it is not a right of way.

In the field go left, back on your original line, to follow the edge of this very large field all the way to its end at a corner and step stile. Crossing into a smaller field go forward with the left fence to a double stile in the next corner. Entering another field go left the short distance to its corner and then swing right to follow the left hedge. Quickly pass and ignore a gated step stile on the left, which carries a crossing path, and stay with the Illey Way path that rises and follows the left hedge. Stay with the hedge and way as it rises to a stiled gateway. In the next field stay with the hedge to arrive at a gated step stile onto Newtown Lane.

Turn right along Newtown Lane to quickly meet a T-junction. Here go left and cross the now rural M5. On the other side go past the turning into Chapmans Hill and take the next right turn into the car park of Waseley Hills Country Park.

Partly public land and partly National Trust, the Country Park is administered by Hereford & Worcester County Council and consists of 150 acres of pasture and woodland. There are toilets, a cafe, information centre and children's play area. From the toposcope on Windmill Hill you have a spectacular 360 degree panorama which takes in the Cotswolds, the Malverns and many more surrounding hills as well as the conurbation you have left behind. Whilst you have freedom to roam within the bounds of the Park the now described route follows public rights of way.

Passing immediately left of the Information Centre go through the waymarked kissing gate in the fence ahead. Walk up the sloping field to take either set of steps up a low embankment and so reach the toposcope on the crest of Windmill Hill.

Leaving the toposcope behind, continue forward with the right hand fence, immediately ignoring a stile in it, to soon arrive alongside a marker post at a wide, made gap in the fence. In the gap there is a fence stile that takes you into an enclosed path that follows your same direction and descends to a step stile which takes you out of the enclosed section and so over a crossing path. Continue forward with a right hedged embankment, on a terraced track, to meet a stranded stile and a 'horseshoe' marker post above farm buildings left.

Follow the horseshoe marker posts forward with a left-hand hedge/fence. Soon arriving at another made gap in the left hedge go left through it and through the left hand kissing gate. Now walk forward with the left hedge to and through another kissing gate. Maintain your way forward and up with the left hedge/fence and at its end continue forward with the embankment path to pass through the remains of a hedgerow into another field. In this field – there is a school and its playing field below and left – go half right (210 degrees) to crest the field. Below, and well left of a field corner where a fence joins a hedge, there is a bench seat in front of a metal kissing gate and a public footpath sign. Walk down to it.

Again you now have good views across the motorway and Worcestershire to the Habberley Hills and the Malverns.

Pass through the kissing gate and walk down two fields with the left hedge/fence. In the second field, just a few feet before the end of the hedge/fence, there is a signpost and another kissing gate – go left through it.

Now follow the right hedge/fence to then leave it and walk down to a signpost on a concrete farm road. Here cross the road at the signpost and make for the step stile in the hedge left of a white house. This takes you onto Redhill Lane where you turn right.

Follow Redhill Lane down to the next turning on the right which is a narrow lane leading to Manor Farm. Here go right to pass the farm yard and go through a gate into a hedged green lane.

This farm has a farm shop where, apart from the usual produce, you can buy an ice-cream!

In a few yards this unsurfaced lane splits – one going right and up, the other (yours) going forward and through a left hand gate. Go through and in a little way, just before the green lane narrows, go left over a waymarked step stile into a young, narrow and enclosed plantation. With the left fence walk forward for its length to a step stile out. In the field follow the right hedge to its protruding corner and then cut the corner to continue forward to the tunnel under the motorway.

Pass through the tunnel and on the other side swing left to pass through a gate into a field. In the field go right to walk parallel to the stream (right) and so reach the next corner where a step stile takes you onto the A491 at a lay-by.

Cross the road into Wildmoor Lane opposite which you follow until reaching a junction near the 'Wildmoor Oak' pub. Here go right into Top Road and immediately left into the pub overflow car park. In front you will see a waymarked and gated step stile which takes you into a field. In the field go diagonally right to cross to the far right corner where there is a fence stile. Over this go forward between a garden fence and a pool where, at the end of the pool, there is a waymarked step stile. Cross it to follow a path forward to another step stile onto a roughly surfaced track. Cross the step stile opposite and then another step stile to follow an enclosed path. This will bring you to yet another step stile after which you follow the right hand fence to reach a lane on a bend.

At the lane go forward (right) to a right bend at the white Mill Cottage. Follow the lane around the bend and stay with it for approximately another three-quarters of a mile until reaching a white metal barrier and railed steps that lead up the left hand embankment. Follow the steps up into an enclosed path along a field edge – *a very good view point* – and so enter a recreation ground. Continue with the right edge to pass the pavilion and so gain the Stourbridge Road in Fairfield.

Here go right and then first left along Wood Lane, a signed 'no through road'. Follow the lane for half a mile as it goes from surfaced to roughly surfaced and then meets the edge of Pepper Wood. Here the lane continues forward as a concreted drive but you go left on the wide, ash track – signed 'Public Bridleway-Dordale Road ½' – to pass through vehicle barriers. Follow this main track as it descends gently through the woodland to meet Dordale Road.

Purchased by the Woodland Trust in 1981, Pepper Wood is a beautiful deciduous woodland – a remnant of the ancient Forest of Feckenham – forming part of a wooded area which is documented as early as the thirteenth century. It probably owes its name to Pyppa, the father of Penda – a Mercian King during the seventh century.

At the road take the track opposite which is signed 'Public Bridleway-Warbage Lane ¾' and 'Royal Content Farm'. Follow the track between barn conversions and right of the old farmhouse – *another of the places the King is reputed to have rested* – to a gate into a field. In this sloping field simply follow the top left hedge through more fields until reaching Warbage Lane at the side of a new house.

Go right along Warbage Lane and immediately left along Woodland Road to enter the environs of Dodford – a fascinating village.

Though Dodford's history goes back many centuries its uniqueness is relatively modern. A glance at the map suggests a uniformly planned settlement – which is exactly what Dodford is for it was created by the Chartists, a nineteenth century reformist movement that sought to settle townsfolk on land of their own so that they would qualify for the franchise. The movement was led by one Feargus O'Connor and in Dodford the settlers were granted a cottage and a smallholding of about four acres. Because of its planned creation the village does not have an identifiable centre but it does enjoy a sense of space with quiet, narrow lanes and hedgerows. In recent years many of the Chartist cottages have been modernised and extended, though there are still examples of the original dwellings to be seen. The views from hereabouts are quite outstanding.

Continuing along Woodland Road, take the first left down Church Road to cross over Victoria Road and so arrive at a T-junction in front of the village hall. Cross over to pass immediately left of the village hall and so follow an enclosed path forward to eventually meet a step stile into a sloping field. In the field go up with the right hand hedge to a step stile onto a narrow lane. Cross over the opposite step stile, quickly followed by another, and walk down the steep bank to a stream in the valley bottom. Here a footbridge takes you over the stream to follow an obvious path up the opposite embankment. Arriving at the top a double fence stile takes you into a field. Cross the field, very slightly left, to a stile in the opposite hedge. Do not cross this stile however instead go right, keeping the hedge on your left, to the field corner where there is a gated double step stile. Over into the next field go forward and across to the far corner, just left of corrugated outbuildings. Here there is a gated step stile onto a road.

Cross the road to the signed step stile opposite. Over this go slightly right to immediately cross another step stile into a paddock where you now follow the rear of the stables through more paddocks. At the end of the paddocks simply follow the same line, with a left hedge/fence, over a series of stiles until reaching steps up to the car park behind the 'Park Gate' pub. Join the car park and then bear right along the service road to join the A448. Here go left and then first right along Monsieurs Hall Lane.

Near this junction is Battlefield Farm which, according to a local publication, earned its name from a skirmish between patrols prior to, or during, the 1651 Battle of Worcester. It is said that a prisoner was put against a sandstone wall and shot at with a cannon. The shot missed and left a hole in the wall which can still be seen near Park Gate – though I have been unable to locate it. It is not recorded whether the prisoner survived either the blast or the shock!

Walk up Monsieurs Hall Lane and eventually pass, on the left, the partly timbered Monsieurs Hall itself. Soon after the hall you will meet 'Upland Cottage' on the right. Here, in the left hedge, there is a waymarked step stile into a sloping field. Cross it and in the field walk forward and down to the far corner where there is a gate left and right. Go through the right hand one and forward with a left hedge/fence to quickly pass through another gate. In this next field continue with the left hedge/fence to meet a gate onto the A448.

On the road go right and pass under the motorway bridge. Immediately on the other side go right over a gated fence stile to initially walk parallel with the motorway – up to your left is the Pine Lodge Hotel. Passing through a gateway in the opposite fence now bear gently left to walk between the remains of a hedge left and a stream right. In a little while the stream gives way to a hedge on the right which you follow to a stile onto a road.

Opposite is Echells Close which you cross to. Now follow the surfaced pavement between a recreation field right and houses left. Stay with this pavement until coming into a cul-de-sac where your path becomes en-closed, passing right of a house, to then meet the perimeter fence of a public park. Follow the fence to the A448 where you go right to follow it into Bromsgrove. At the mini-island just past The Perry Hall Hotel bear right (Hanover Street) and then right again (Worcester Road) to 'Ye Olde Black Cross'.

This early seventeenth century inn is another of the many places where Charles is said to have hidden. However, on this occasion, the King may well have taken refreshment here for we know that his horse needed to be re-shod in Bromsgrove.

Ye Olde Black Cross

15

BROMSGROVE to HEADLESS CROSS

10 miles

With his horse now shod the King's party continued their journey to Stratford upon Avon.

MAPS: Landranger (1:50,000) 139 & 150; Pathfinder (1;25,000) 953, 974 & 975.
PARKING: Public Car Parks in Bromsgrove. Roadside near the Methodist Church, Headless Cross, or near Morton Stanley Park.
TOURIST INFORMATION: Bromsgrove (01527 31809) Redditch (01527 60806).
START: Ye Olde Black Cross, Bromsgrove (GR 957704).
FINISH: Headless Cross Methodist Church (Redditch) (GR 038658) or B4504 road at GR 030653.

FROM 'Ye Olde Black Cross' continue along Worcester Road to turn left along Charford Road. At the end of this road you will come to traffic lights on the dual carriageway by-pass. Cross over to follow Stoke Road for half a mile and immediately past 'The Dragoon' pub turn right along St. Godwalds Road. In a few yards cross a railway bridge and on the other side immediately turn left over a step stile to follow an enclosed path alongside the railway. In a while this will bring you to a road on a bend.

Go right for about 75 yards where on the right and after the last house you will see a signed footpath for Walnut Lane. Turn right onto this enclosed footpath and follow it to cross a stile into a field. Now following the left fence enter a second and then a third field when the fence swings gently left through a fourth and brings you to an enclosed path at woodland. Follow this to a lane and turn right to soon reach cross-roads.

Here go left along Dusthouse Lane for just over half a mile (passing London Lane) until it makes a sharp left turn. At the bend leave the lane to continue forward into a field where you follow the remains of concrete posts and a series of manholes. At the last post go half right across the field to pass immediately left of a shrub covered mound. Past the mound continue your line across the narrow neck of the field to join the right hand stream at a footbridge. Cross over and on the other side go forward on an enclosed path which in turn brings you to a step stile. Over this continue forward and up to meet a step stile, next to a garden fence, which takes you onto a road. Here go right and follow the road, past the entrance to the British Waterways offices, and so over the canal. On the other side turn right and walk down to the canal side – *behind you is the Tardebigge Tunnel entrance* – and now follow the towpath to the lock keepers cottage.

Immediately before the cottage there is a step stile on the left which you cross into a sloping field. Here go forward and up aiming just right of the church spire – St. Bartholomew's. *The church and its hill top is a prominent vantage point with many good views around.* On this line cross two more step stiles and so arrive at a crossing tarmac path immediately in front of the church school.

Turn right along this path and then in a short distance go left across the grass to pass between the end of a rusty corrugated iron building and a hedgerow. Following the hedgerow along the edge of the school play area reach a step stile onto a road.

The next mile follows footpath No.6 – Bentley Pauncefoot Parish. At the time of writing this path was totally devoid of signs, stiles and waymarks

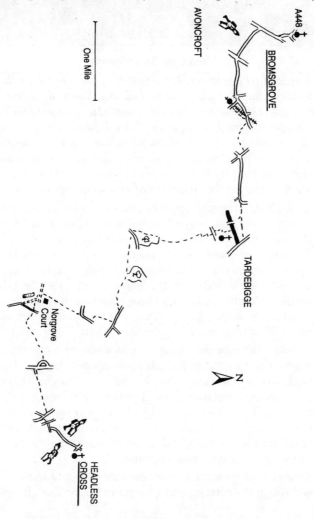

Tardebigge Tunnel portal

for the whole of its length – GR 99556890 to GR 99406725. It was also obstructed in a couple of places by barbed wire. You will see from the map that it also makes several turns and this, coupled with some of the hedgerows having disappeared, made navigation a little difficult. These problems have been fully reported to Hereford & Worcester County Council so that hopefully, by the time this book is published, the necessary remedial actions will have been taken. The following then is the route at the time of writing though do look out for the possibility of new stiles, signs and waymarks.

Cross the road to the gate opposite and enter a field. Ahead of you is a line of three oak trees which you follow (on the right) to the last one. Here turn right and cross the field to the protruding corner of the opposite hedge. Arriving there continue the few yards into the inverted corner and cross over the barbed wire fence to go left through a small hedge gap and the remains of a fence or stile. In the field go left for the short distance to the nearest corner where you then swing right to follow the left hedge to the next corner. Here swing right again, still following the left hedge, and in just under 50 yards come to a gate, on the left.

Pass through the gate into another field where you now have another field crossing, slightly right, to the gate in the opposite hedge – 140 degrees. Go through this gate into another field where you cut the corner by going half right to the section of barbed wire fencing in a hedge gap – 200 degrees. Cross this fence (there is a gate nearby – if needed) and maintain the same line across this next field, under power lines, to a gate. Entering another field again cross the centre (170 degrees) to pass close to double wooden power poles and so reach a gate opposite.

In the next field go left the short distance to a gate in the corner. Do not pass through the gate, instead go right to follow the left hedge all the way to the edge of woodland. At the trees go right and then left to follow the woodland edge all the way to ranch fencing at Banks Green Farm.

Cross this fencing and walk forward to the right hand of two white gates. Through this pass right (rear) of wooden stables and at the protruding corner of the fence go half left to the farthest left corner of the field to pass over more ranch fencing and immediately through another white gate next to an oak tree. In another field go immediately left for the few yards to the corner where the remains of a stile take you onto a road.

On the road cross over to the step stile in the opposite hedge. Entering the field go diagonally left (due east) to meet the left hedge at a footbridge and step stile. Cross into the neighbouring field and continue pretty much the same line (100 degrees) to meet a right hand hedge. At the hedge go left to follow it to the next corner where there is a step stile. Cross over to continue forward along the edge of the next field (trees left) to the next corner where there is (right of a gate) a fence stile immediately followed by a footbridge and a step stile. Go over these into the next field and maintain your line forward with the left hedge to the next corner. Here, just a few yards right of the corner, there is a step stile into yet another field. Still following the left hedge follow this field to pass through a gateway. Staying with the left hedge/fence follow it the short distance to its protruding corner where you leave it to cross the field to a gate onto a lane, just left of the new Webheath Pumping Station.

On the lane go right and follow it up to the 30 mph signs – just before Foxlydiates Lane – where you go acutely right on a tarmac track, quickly passing an ivy covered house and arriving at a gated fence stile. Over and forward pass right of a block building, on the remains of the tarmac track, to meet a field gate. Through into the next field follow the right hedge down to another gate through which you immediately pass through another into a sloping field. Walk up with the left hedge to enter another field where you go left to a recessed corner, a stile and a footpath sign.

Cross over onto a surfaced lane and go right, down to a right hand bend. Do not take the left hand bridleway sign at the bend but go on just a few yards further to a footpath sign, also on the left. Here cross the fence stile into a field corner where you are faced with a centre field crossing. Go straight ahead aiming for the double wooden power poles (200 degrees). On reaching them continue down the field, following the power lines, to the protruding corner of the hedge/fence in front. Here there is a step stile which you cross into another field to leave the power lines and go half right aiming for the far-most left corner – 220 degrees. Arriving there cross a step stile and in the next field continue forward with the left hedge – ahead you can see Norgrove Court. Passing through a gate follow the same hedge which will eventually take you right of Norgrove Court to a gate.

Go through the gate to T-junction with a crossing track. Here go left through another gate, towards the Court, and quickly arrive at a wrought iron gate. Do not go through this one, instead go right through the wooden hunter's gate to follow the short enclosed path to the main gates and a

Norgrove Court – another reputed royal resting place!

cattle grid. Turn right along the tarmac drive and in only a few yards go left through a fence gate into a sloping pasture. Now go straight ahead up the slope to the opposite fence where there is a step stile left of a gate. Cross over and quickly cross another stile onto a lane. Opposite is a field gate, with a public footpath sign for Green Lane and Elcocks Brook, which you pass through into a field.

Walk forward and down the field with the right hand hedge and follow it for about three quarters of its length. Now go half left across the field to the bottom left corner where there is a fence stile. Cross this and the two-step stile immediately on the left into the bottom of another field. Ignoring the step stile and footbridge just a few feet in front, walk forward along the bottom edge of this field with the stream on your right.

In the next corner cross a gated fence stile and continue following the stream to meet another gated fence stile. Over this again follow the stream to yet another fence stile into yet another field. Continue forward parallel to the stream to arrive at an oak tree in the protruding corner of ranch fencing. At the oak tree go forward with the fence on your right to a step stile in the inverted corner. Cross over and go left with the fence to meet a stile onto a lane at a bend. Go right along the lane to T-junction with a road. Here turn right and then left into the Morton Stanley Park.

Passing in front of the changing rooms take the tarmac path forward to follow a generally easterly direction – keeping the wooded slopes on your right – for about a third of a mile until reaching a road, the B4504.

If you wish, this section can be ended at this point – there is car parking nearby – but the description continues into Headless Cross for those who need shops and other services.

At the road go right and then left to pass under the road via a subway. Take the right fork in the path to meet another road. Here cross over into Swinburne Road and follow it forward to another subway. Do not go under it, instead go left with the path up to bungalows on Mason Road. Here go left and follow Mason Road up for half a mile to a mini-island where you turn right along Evesham Road towards the Methodist Church spire.

16

HEADLESS CROSS to ALCESTER

9½ miles

And so they continued to Stratford-upon-Avon.

MAPS: Landranger (1:50,000) 150; Pathfinder (1:25,000) 975 & 997.
PARKING: Roadside near the Methodist Church, Headless Cross, or near Morton Stanley Park. Public car parks in Alcester.
ALONG THE WAY: The Old Malt House, Alcester.
TOURIST INFORMATION: Redditch (01527 60806).
START: Headless Cross Methodist Church (Redditch) (GR 038658), or B4504 road at GR 030653.
FINISH: Parish Church, High Street, Alcester (GR 091575).

FROM Headless Cross Methodist Church retrace your steps north-west along Evesham Road to the mini-island. Here turn left and follow Mason Road all the way down to Swinburne Road where you turn right to follow it to a T-junction. Cross over the road and follow the surfaced footpath and the power lines to pass under a subway. On the other side, in front, is a house which used to be the farmhouse to Walkwood Farm. Go right along the footpath and then immediately left through a wooden fence gap. This takes you onto the old lane on the right side of the old farm buildings.

Go forward and up the old lane (Morton Lane) with new houses left and woodland right. In a while you will T-junction with Callow Hill Lane where you turn right to pass 'Windmill Cottage' when, a few yards beyond, you will see a public footpath sign on the left. Here go left through the gate to pass right of stables and immediately through another gate. After this second gate, immediately in front is a broken gate with a step stile. Over this go up the sloping field with the fence to your left.

Cresting the field you will have outstanding views of the Habberley and Malvern Hills.

Descending from the crest of the field, with the left hedge, you will find a step stile in the bottom corner. Cross this into a hedged green lane where you turn left to follow it to a surfaced lane. Here go left again to soon pass the original Tudor and very attractive, Lovelyne Farm. Next pass 'Lane Cottage' just after which you will see a footpath sign on the left which is pointing right. Here go right over a step stile next to a gate and go forward with the right hand hedge along a narrow pasture. Arriving in a corner cross a step stile and a footbridge where you swing left to enter a field.

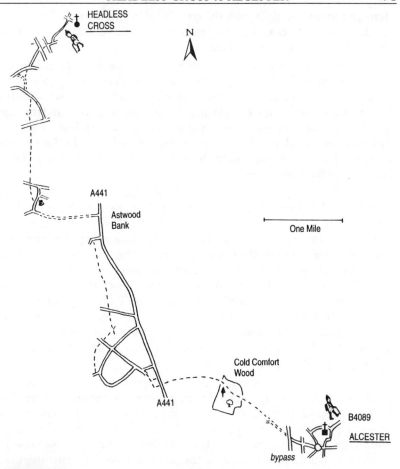

Lovelyne Farm

Here go forward, initially with the right hand hedge, to cross this natural meadow. Go over a crossing grassy track to maintain your line and so reach a step stile in the top, far right corner.

Cross over into another field. *Super views again here.* Turn left and follow the left hedge to the first corner where you cross a step stile to the drive in front of the gates to 'The Mount'. Go right and down with the drive to a lane. At the lane go right and then left (signed) down and through the gate to Chapel House Farm. Passing right of the farmhouse continue with the drive which now has ranch fencing. Immediately the drive makes a left bend where you turn right through a wicket gate and immediately over a fence stile into a field.

In the field go straight ahead to a footbridge at a protruding hedge corner. On the other side and in another field go forward (south), across the centre, to a gap in the opposite hedge. This will bring you to a bridged stream where you go over a gated fence stile. Now swing right and head south again for the step stile in the fence ahead. Over this stile you will see a derelict wind pump in front, however you swing left away from it and towards the nearest field corner where there is a single strand barbed wire fence. Just above the corner there is a 'cushioned' crossing point onto a fenced track. Cross the track to the step in the gate opposite and so enter another field. Here go forward and up to pass under telegraph wires at the lowest point of the slope. Ahead you will see a line of oak trees which lead you to a step stile onto a tarmac lane.

Cross the lane to the signed fence stile opposite and so into a narrow paddock. Now cross the fence stile just a few yards ahead into a field. In the field continue forward and across it to the opposite hedge/fence where an oak tree is your aiming point – 160 degrees. At the oak tree cross a footbridge and a fence stile into the next field which you now cross by going very slightly right to a gap in the far corner. At the corner there is a gated step stile. Cross into the next field and go sharply left for the short distance to a gate onto a road opposite Astwood Court.

Go right along the road and ignoring footpath signs right and left stay a few yards more with the road until reaching a right hand bend. On the right there is a bridleway sign pointing left directly to the ornamental, automatic, gates for 'Astwood Farm' and 'Windy Bank'. Press the button on the right hand side of the gates and go through to follow the concrete road/bridleway up to and left of the very old and attractive Astwood Farmhouse.

Just past the farmhouse you will pass through a gateway and immediately draw level with four hoppers on the right. To the left there are two adjacent gates. Leave the concrete to go left and through the right hand of the two gates. Ignoring another gate on the left quickly pass through double gates in front and so enter a field. Now follow the right hedge/fence up to the top corner where there is a gated step stile. In the next field continue up to the next corner and pass through a gate onto an enclosed path which quickly brings you to another gate. Through this join the tarmac road, right of Doebank House, and follow it forward as it joins another road to continue the same direction and so join the A441 (Evesham Road) at Astwood Bank.

Go right along the A441 and then turn right along Edgioake Lane (B4092 – signed Inkberrow) where just a short distance in you will see a footpath sign on the left for 'Saltway 1'. This takes you over a stile and into an enclosed path between the houses. *You now follow this path in a generally southerly direction for about a mile.*

Beyond the houses the path follows the edge of nurseries and then enters a field where you follow the top edge with the hedge left. In the next corner cross a step stile and then three more stiles in close proximity. Under power lines go left to a wooden kissing gate through which you turn immediately right to follow the other side of the hedge. Go through another kissing gate and so forward again under another set of power lines – indeed under the pylon itself where you will find another kissing gate in the corner which is immediately followed by a step stile. In the next field continue forward with the right hand fence and in the next corner cross another step stile. Immediately on your right is a gated step stile which you cross to resume your southerly direction, now with the fence/hedge on your left.

Just before the next corner of this field there is another step stile in the left fence/hedge which you cross to go right again (south) with the hedge/fence now on your right. At the next corner go through a gate into a hedged green lane and so quickly meet a road.

Cross the road to the signed step stile opposite and in the field walk forward with the right hand hedge/fence, quickly passing a pool. In the next corner there is a step stile right and a fence stile in front, cross the one in front. Soon cross a double fence stile in the next corner and in the next field continue forward with the right hedge/fence. This will take you immediately left of a second pool and so under the power lines at the next corner.

Here there are footbridges forward and right. Cross the right hand – more substantial – bridge into a field corner. Now, with the left hedge/fence, walk forward along the bottom of three fields to arrive at a tarmac lane left of Hookey's Farm. Opposite is what looks like a hedged drive but in fact leads you into a field via a gate. In the field follow the left hedge to a gate in the next corner. Through this pass left of a gas pipeline compound to enter another field. Here go right to follow the field edge for about 125 yards when you will see a blue metal gate on your right – go through it. In the next field turn immediately left to follow the left hedge/fence all the way to a gate onto a surfaced lane.

On the lane go left the short distance to a junction. Here turn right and follow this lane (Lower Cladswell Lane), through the attractive hamlet of Cladswell, all the way to a T-junction. At the junction go right and follow the road up to a sharp left bend. Do not follow the road bend, instead continue forward along the unsurfaced road between houses and so left of the entrance to 'Lambrook' to meet a public footpath sign at 'Lilac End'.

The sign directs you into an enclosed path for Oak Tree Lane. Follow it through two kissing gates to arrive at the gravel lane.

Now turn left for 12 yards to then go right through the kissing gate next to the entrance for 'Russet Lawns'. This enclosed path soon brings you into the end of a cul-de-sac. Continue forward for about 15 yards and then go left along the signed and enclosed footpath that passes between the second and third bungalows. This will bring you up to the A441 again.

On the other side of the main road is a signed bridleway for Alcester – join it. Follow it down between conifers left and a fence right into a small field. *Ahead are outstanding views across Warwickshire – which you have just entered.* Continue down for a few yards to the bottom right corner where you go right down a bank to swing left and forward along an enclosed track. This will bring you into a field where you follow its edge, firstly with woodland on your right and then a hedge, almost to the bottom corner. Just before this bottom corner there is a waymarked oak tree on the right. Go right at the tree and then quickly left along a clear, enclosed path. In a little while this will bring you to a step stile which you cross into a field corner.

Now walk forward through a fence gap and follow the left fence for some way until coming to its end at a protruding corner. Just a short distance ahead you will see the gate into Coldharbour Wood. Walk directly to, and through, it.

In the woodland follow the clear track forward and exit the trees on the other side via a gateway just before a house. Continue forward to pass right of the house on a semi-surfaced track. After a while you will come to a crossing tarmac road which leads to Coldcomfort Farm. Here go left along the tarmac (Coldcomfort Lane) to soon reach the footbridge over the new Alcester by-pass.

On the other side continue forward along Allimore Lane and in a while cross the road bridge over a dismantled railway. Just a short distance in front is a cross-roads which you go over to follow Seggs Lane, past the Fire Station, and so reach a traffic island. On the other side follow Swan Street for a few yards to turn first left into High Street. Follow High Street up to St. Nicholas' Parish Church and the end of this section.

Alcester is a most interesting town to explore. Apart from its Roman connections it has several old buildings of particular architectural merit.

17

ALCESTER to WOOTTON WAWEN

7 miles

And still making for Stratford-upon-Avon...

MAPS: Landranger (1;50,000) 150 & 151; Pathfinder
(1:25,000) 975 & 997.
PARKING: Public Car Park in Alcester. Roadside in Wootton
Wawen.
ALONG THE WAY: Kinwarton Dovecote (NT) nearby. Wootton
Wawen Hall and Church.
TOURIST INFORMATION: Redditch (01527 60806) Alcester
(Public Library – 01789 762430) Stratford-upon-Avon
(01789 293127).
START: Parish Church, High Street, Alcester (GR 091575).
FINISH: Parish Church, on A3400, in Wootton Wawen
(GR 154632).

FACING the church (north) pass to its right and follow the B4089 out of town, soon crossing the River Arrow by way of Gunnings Bridge. Stay with the B4089 (keeping on the left) for another half a mile where, about 100 yards after passing Kinwarton Farm Road, you turn left along a waymarked, enclosed footpath which is also signed as the Heart of England Way.

The Heart of England Way is a long distance regional footpath that travels 100 miles from Cannock Chase to Bourton-on-the-Water in the Cotswolds.

Following this path will eventually bring you to a step stile into a field. Here go straight ahead over the brow to a triangulation pillar at 216 feet. Continue forward to pass right of a small clump of bushes in the middle of the field and so reach a gated step stile in a fence. Over this go left through a short, narrow section of fencing to another waymarked step stile. Cross it and go forward 'over' a brick bridge that 'spans' a disused and filled-in railway line. On the other side cross a step stile into a field corner where you continue forward and up the field with the left hand hedge. *Good views around.*

At the brow of the field, and before overhead power lines, go left over a step stile in the hedge. On the other side go right to continue your line but now with the hedge on your right. Quickly reaching the near corner cross another step stile and carry on forward to pass under the power lines and reach another step stile in the next corner. Over this and into another field continue forward, still with the right hand hedge, all the way to gates onto a road.

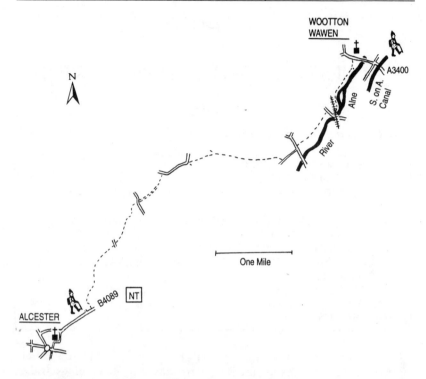

On the road go left for some 25 yards where on the right you will see a waymarked step stile. Cross it into a field and walk forward up the slope to a stile in the hedge near a top corner – when you arrive there you will see that the stile is left of a pool. Over the stile go forward a few yards through scrub vegetation to a crossing dirt track. Follow the track right for 30 yards when you will see a marker post on the left. Go to it and follow the clear path through young trees until arriving in a field corner.

In the field continue forward with the right hedge for something like a third of a mile and follow it through a gradual left bend to a gap between two oak trees – this is just before the protruding hedge corner. Go right between the two closely placed oak trees, into the adjacent field where you go left to follow the field edge around a right bend. This will bring you to a field corner immediately before a house. Just a few feet before the corner and the house there is a plank footbridge and step stile on the left – cross them and turn immediately right into the corner next to the house. In the corner cross another plank footbridge into the end of a meadow/garden. Go forward along the bottom edge for just a short distance and then right over a step stile onto a road.

Follow the road left for 25 yards and then go right along the unsurfaced road to 'Dinglewell Farm' and 'Larkshill'. Soon passing the entrance to 'Larkshill' continue with the road/track to pass left of an isolated detached house and over a cattle grid. Now continue a few yards further forward to a point under power lines. Here, on the left, there is a gated step stile –

cross it. In the field go diagonally right, on an obvious track, up to a gated step stile. Over this continue forward along the edge of the field with the right hedge. In the next corner cross a step stile onto a road.

Here you leave the Heart of England Way.

Go right along the road and follow it for a little under half a mile – passing Woodhouse Farm and Crocketts Farm on the way – to 'Glebe Farm' where the road makes a sharp left turn. Do not follow the road around the bend but instead go forward, right of 'Glebe Farm', on a short, waymarked track into a field corner. Here rights of way go right and left. You take the left one down the field edge with a hedge on the left. In the bottom corner you will come to double gates and a step stile. Cross the stile to continue your same direction but now with the ditch and hedge on your right. Follow this path/track for just over half a mile where it crosses the ditch and continues forward in the same direction but with the ditch and hedge now on your left. Follow it all the way to a gated step stile onto the B4089.

Turn left along the road and follow it for a quarter of a mile, through Little Alne, to a sharp left bend and a junction. Here follow the left bend (signed Wootton Wawen) and just around it, immediately after a large road sign, go right over a gated step stile. In the field walk forward (north-east) and up with the left hand fence to the top left corner. Here cross a gated fence stile and maintain your line up this second field to the opposite hedge and another fence stile. Over this into a third field go straight ahead and down, aiming for a hedge gap which is just left of a farm house. Arriving at the gap cross a fence stile and a concrete footbridge onto a narrow lane in front of Grey Mill Farm.

On the lane go left for about 15 yards and then right to a waymarked stile. In a field go diagonally left across it aiming just left of a low brick building. This will bring you to a step stile. In the next field go straight ahead on a line for the far right corner where a step stile takes you onto a lane.

Follow the lane right to pass under a railway bridge and, immediately before the river bridge, go left over a cattle grid and through a gate to follow the concrete road towards the water treatment plant. At the third telegraph pole on the left, swing a little right to cut the corner of the pasture and so reach the protruding right corner of the perimeter fence around the plant. Now walking between the perimeter fence (left) and the River Alne (right), cross a series of stiles to stay with the river bank until reaching the second of two bridges crossing the river.

Do not cross this second bridge – which is a footbridge – instead swing left and up to a waymarked fence to then follow an elevated path towards Wootton Wawen church ahead. Pass the remnants of an isolated kissing gate and joining a wall pass through another kissing gate onto tarmac. Go forward and up to shortly reach the A3400 in front of the ornamental gates to Wootton Hall – the end of this section.

There is plenty to see in Wootton Wawen which has a convenient shop and pub.

18

WOOTTON WAWEN to STRATFORD-UPON-AVON

10 miles

Just a short distance from Stratford-upon-Avon the royal party came upon a group of Parliamentarian troopers who were resting their horses at the roadside. Leaving the road they avoided contact only to meet the same troop again in Stratford: this time avoidance was not possible and they could only go forward to pass the mounted soldiers. This was achieved without incident.

> MAPS: Landranger (1:50,000) 151; Pathfinder (1:25,000) 975,976,997 & 998.
> PARKING: Side roads in Wootton Wawen. Public car Parks in Stratford-upon-Avon.
> ALONG THE WAY: Wootton Wawen Hall and Church. The Obelisk on Welcombe Hill. The Royal Shakespeare Theatre.
> TOURIST INFORMATION: Stratford-upon-Avon (01789 293127).
> START: Wootton Wawen (GR 153632).
> FINISH: Royal Shakespeare Theatre, Stratford-upon-Avon (GR 204548).

FROM the centre of Wootton Wawen go east along the A3400 to soon reach the cast iron aqueduct that carries the Stratford-upon-Avon Canal over the road. Pass under the aqueduct to immediately go right

Wootton Hall

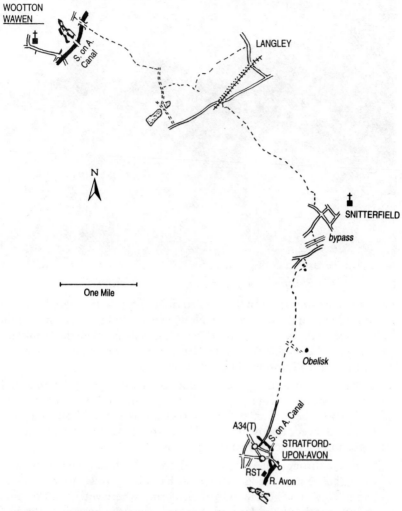

and up to join the towpath at the cast iron 'trough'. Go left (north) along the towpath at the side of the 'trough'.

The canal was opened in 1831 and this aqueduct is one of its most striking features. The towpath is such that as you follow it your head is in line with the water level! Some years back the canal fell into severe decay and its outstanding beauty was almost lost for ever. However the National Trust – with many volunteers – eventually undertook its restoration and after many years hard work it became navigable – and walkable – once more. More recently it was handed back to British Waterways.

Follow the towpath until reaching the third bridge (51) where you cross the canal to now follow a hedged bridleway in a south-easterly direction. After some distance the bridleway follows the left edge of woodland and then further on begins a gentle rise. Just beyond the top of the rise it merges with a public footpath coming in from the right and then swings left to a

The Stratford-upon-Avon Canal near Wootton Wawen

hunter's gate into a field. In the field go right to follow the woodland edge and quickly reach the field corner. Now turn left and walk down with the right hedge all the way to Cutlers Farm. Here walk between the farmhouse (right) and the outbuildings and barn conversions (left) to reach a T-junction with a crossing, surfaced, farm road.

At the junction turn right and follow the road beyond the buildings. Ignoring a bridleway sign pointing left continue forward with the now hedged road where soon the hedgerows are left behind and the road becomes unfenced. Following this pleasant road, pass an isolated gate on the right and then soon arrive at a gateway on the left.

Turn left through the gateway and cross the bridged ditch to walk forward and up a field edge with a left hand hedgerow. After cresting a second brow you will come to the field corner where you go left through a gap into another field. Here go forward along the bottom of the field with a right hedge/fence. In the next corner is a gate which you pass through to enter an enclosed track. Follow the track forward (right) as it gently rises and then widens into a green lane. Soon it will bring you to the surfaced road in the centre of Langley village opposite the tiny church of St. Mary.

Turn right to follow the village road. At a ford sign join the enclosed path that travels a few feet parallel to the road and cross the footbridge over the ford. Shortly rejoin the road itself and follow it forward, passing under a railway bridge, to a T-junction. Here go right and follow the road .(signed Bearley & Stratford) to a point immediately in front of another railway bridge.

Avid map readers will probably have noticed that I have diverted from a more direct route to follow this one through Langley village. This is quite deliberate for at the time of writing a bridleway that fords a fairly deep stream, to then meet the second railway bridge, has no footbridge for walkers. Likewise, the footpath that runs parallel to the railway and joins the two railway bridges was obstructed by fencing and undergrowth – though over the coming months and years this may well change.

Nonetheless Langley is a pleasant place to be and combines a tasteful mix of ancient and modern dwellings along quiet roads. As the additional distance walked is negligible, I suspect most people will prefer the described route anyway.

In front of this second railway bridge a track goes off left. Follow it and in a few yards go through the gate in front and so enter a long and narrow field. Here go immediately left to follow the left hand hedge all the way to the next corner. Now pass through a gap and continue forward along the edge of another field – still with a left hand hedge – to arrive at the inverted corner of woodland. Now maintaining your line enter the trees to follow a just discernible path up through the trees. Crossing right of the end of a muddy depression bear left to follow its upper edge and so continue rising near to the right edge of the woodland. Near its end the path becomes clearer and meets the perimeter fence of a golf course. Follow the fence to immediately leave it and enter the corner of a field.

In the field go left to then swing right with a rounded corner and so resume your original line now with the hedge/fence on your left. Following the hedge/fence for this and two more fields will bring you into a fourth where the hedge/fence is now on your right.

These fields follow a contour edge that offers lovely views across this part of rolling Warwickshire.

In the next corner of this fourth field a footbridge awaits to take you into a fifth. Over the bridge go left to arrive at a step stile just right of the next corner. Crossing the stile go right along the edge of a sports field to the next corner where you cross another step stile into an enclosed path. Follow this to a road (Bearley Road) on the edge of Snitterfield.

A fairly large village, Snitterfield is another community of mixed dwellings with several of the houses dating from Tudor times. William Shakespeare's grandfather, Richard, farmed land near to the church and it is interesting to note that he rented the farm from a John Arden of Wilmcote who was the father of Mary – the bard's mother.

Turn left along Bearley Road to pass the Snitterfield Arms and the school to reach a cross roads. Go right along 'The Green' and follow this through an older part of the village. Immediately before the speed de-restriction signs at the village edge go left along a tarmac drive (there is a very old footpath sign in the hedge) to meet a gate and the remains of a kissing gate on the right, just before the first cottage. Go through the kissing gate and follow the enclosed path forward to eventually meet another kissing gate which takes you into an orchard. Go up the edge of the orchard with the right hedge/fence to and through a wooden kissing gate onto the new by-pass road. Carefully crossing the by-pass take the steps up the opposite bank and go through another kissing gate. Continue forward for the short distance necessary to reach a final kissing gate onto the surfaced Kings Lane.

It is in this lane that the King's first encounter with the troops (referred to above) is believed to have taken place.

Turn right along Kings Lane (quickly passing 'Uporchard' on the left – B & B) and follow it for about 450 yards to arrive at a road sign on the left stating 'Give Way – 150 yds'. Just a few yards before this, also on the left, there is a public footpath marker-post pointing along the drive to 'Snitterfield Fruit Farm', 'Hollow Meadow' and 'Bramley'. Go left along the drive and quickly pass through a gate. Just a few feet beyond the gate go right at a marker post and walk along the edge of an orchard (right) and farm buildings (left).

This will bring you to a gap through high, Leyland cypress trees. Through this continue forward with a block building on the left and orchard to the right along a broad, unsurfaced track. Soon with fruit trees on both sides – *nice views appear to the left and you will also see the obelisk on Welcombe Hill* – your track descends and at the bottom swings left to follow a right hand hedge for about 150 yards to arrive in a corner.

Here go forward through the corner gap and then immediately right through another gap into the top of a field. Turn left and follow the left hedge just a few yards into the corner. Turn right to follow the left hand hedge, in the same field, to the bottom corner where there is a step stile in a fence. Cross over and walk a few feet right to cross a sleeper footbridge into another field.

Walk forward across the centre of this field, just right of the larger of two bushes in front, on a bearing of 170 degrees. This will bring you to a small gap in the opposite hedge which you go through, down a low bank, and so arrive on the edge of a golf course next to a tee. Here pass left of the tee, cross a waymarked footbridge, and walk forward to meet a hedgerow which you follow, keeping it on your left, upwards to meet a gated step stile in the top corner. Cross this into a field and walk up the centre and over the brow aiming for the clump of trees right of the obelisk – your way is in fact assisted by an intermittent line of posts.

Arriving at the opposite hedge/fence cross a step stile and walk forward now with a hedge on your right. Passing under telegraph lines pass through a gate in the next corner and in the next field continue forward again with the hedge on your right to the next corner – and the trees – where there is a gate on the right.

Do not go through this gate – however, remember it for the return – but instead make the diversion now described to view the obelisk.

Turn left to follow a bridleway along the top edge of the field to soon reach a gate leading to the obelisk.

The obelisk is a very large memorial to various members of the Philips family and stands in a very prominent position on the Welcombe Hills with good views around. A toposcope identifies various features through 360 degrees and it is interesting to note that to the east-south-east and twelve miles away is

Edge Hill, scene of the first major battle of the Civil War in 1642. There are also picnic tables and benches here making it an admirable refreshment spot.

Retrace your steps back along the bridleway to the field corner gate identified earlier. Pass through it and turn immediately left along an enclosed path with fence right and trees left. This will bring you to a metal hunter's gate which you pass through to ignore the hunter's gate on the right and continue forward along the top of a rounded ridge. Soon beginning a descent and following a power line your path soon becomes a distinctive track which passes an information notice board and then passes through a hunter's gate at the side of a larger gate into a tarmac lane.

Continuing forward and down you will pass through another gate and then quickly pass the entrance to 'The Wellhouse' immediately after which, and immediately before Clopton Tower, you go left to a gated step stile and so into a field. *The close-by Clopton House was, for a time, the home of Ambrose Rookwood – one of the Gunpowder Plotters.* Passing immediately left of a covered reservoir walk towards the roof tops ahead and down the field centre. Arriving at the left edge of the housing estate pass through a metal kissing gate and follow the tarmac footpath to join Maidenhead Road.

This pleasant residential road takes you forward for some way to the edges of Stratford. Immediately past a row of terraced houses on the left you will come to the road bridge over the Stratford-upon-Avon Canal. Descend to the towpath to go left (south-east) and follow it down past locks and under the next bridge. Here the towpath changes sides and you follow it to pass under another bridge and so reach the attractive basin and lock – within splendid riverside parkland – that connects the canal to the River Avon. At the river go right and follow it downstream to the Royal Shakespeare Theatre and journey's end.

Stratford-upon-Avon needs little introduction and is perhaps the most famous of visitor centres in England. A full day can be spent exploring this handsome town with its many Shakespearean connections.

Stratford-upon-Avon

Camp sites

(Worcester to Stratford-upon-Avon)

Rushock
Mrs S Savage
Little London
Rushock
Droitwich WR9 0NP.
MR 139/887704.
Tel: 01299 23638.

Sutton Maddock
Mrs M Palmer
Sutton Hill Farm
Sutton Maddock
Shifnal
Shropshire.
MR 127/705029.
Tel: 01952 71217.

Stratford
The Stratford-upon-Avon
  Racecourse Camping Site
The Racecourse
Luddington Road
Stratford-upon-Avon
Warwickshire CV37 9SE.
MR 151/186523.
Tel: 01789 267949.

NB. *These are known camp sites that existed at the time of writing. However, changes will inevitably take place and you should check prior to your visit that the owners still offer this service. The facilities offered can range widely from basic to luxury.*

Youth Hostels

Along the complete Way

Ironbridge Gorge
Stratford-upon-Avon
Stow-on-the-Wold
Bristol (Centre)
Bridport
Salisbury
Arundel
Brighton

Useful Addresses

Hereford & Worcester County
Council
Rights of Way Section
Department of Environmental
Services
County Hall
Spetchley Road
WORCESTER
WR5 2NP
Tel: 01905 766876

Dudley Metropolitan Borough
Council
Rights of Way Section
Public Works Department
Council House
Mary Stevens Park
STOURBRIDGE
West Midlands
DY8 2AA
Tel: 01384 453424 Ext. 5424

Staffordshire County Council
Rights of Way Section
Department of Planning and
Economic Development
County Buildings
Martin Street
STAFFORD
ST16 2LE
Tel: 01785 277245

South Staffordshire District Council
Council Offices
Codsall
WOLVERHAMPTON
West Midlands
WV8 1PX
Tel: 01902 6111

Shropshire County Council
Rights of Way Section
Leisure Services Department
Countryside Service
Column House
7 London Road
SHREWSBURY
SY2 6NW
Tel: 01743 255054

Warwickshire County Council
Rights of Way Section
Planning and Transportation
Department
Shire Hall
WARWICK
CV34 4SX
Tel: 01926 412889

British Waterways
Regional Office
Peel's Wharf
Fazeley
TAMWORTH
Staffordshire
B78 3QZ
Tel: 01827 252000

The Ramblers' Association
1/5 Wandsworth Road
LONDON
SW8 2XX
Tel: 0171 582 6878

If, when using this book, you find any obstructions or problems of access on rights of way it would be helpful to report the circumstances to the appropriate county council or local authority, with copies to the Ramblers' Association and to Meridian Books.

Index

Also from Meridian
And the Road Below
by John Westley

The blister-by-blister account of his record breaking walk around the coastline of the British Isles in aid of Multiple Sclerosis

"There are two Cornwalls; one, the rugged coastal Cornwall, home of the equally rugged fisherfolk who hold down more jobs than most people manage in a lifetime – a storm-battered Cornwall that puts on its Sunday best for the multitudinous tourists; and second, the genteel creek and river Cornwall where palm trees outnumber ravens and yachts outnumber fishing boats."

"What a year for nature's bounteous gifts! The hedgerows were a positive riot of edible colour; blackberries, sloes, rosehips and elderberries, all in a state of pristine perfection. Surely the result of a wet spring and an Indian summer, and indicative of a severe winter to come."

"My westerly route now carried me to land-ward of the six mile expanse of Mersehead Sands. Without my cumbersome haversack I might have risked crossing it on foot; with it I had grave reservations as to my ability to outpace the tide which sweeps in at an alarming rate of knots."

"Gusting wind and pelting rain were already in full swing by the time I vacated my digs. Ahead of me lay a clockwise coastal sweep around the north-west corner of the Burren, a 500 square mile lunar landscape of pavement-like limestone slabs crazed with deep fissures and scattered with boulders. An outwardly inhospitable terrain at the best of times, this morning it was positively forbidding."

In August 1990 John Westley commenced what was to become a record breaking walk around the coastline of the British Isles. Sponsored by the Royal Mail, his 'Around the Isles Campaign' in aid of Multiple Sclerosis collected a five figure sum for the Multiple Sclerosis Society as well as giving valuable publicity to the needs of sufferers from this crippling disease, and of their families. Just over a year later his walk was complete, John having walked 9,469 miles (and worn out nine pairs of boots!), thereby earning himself a place in the *Guiness Book of Records*.

His day by day account of his travels are now recounted in this absorbing new book which reveals his joy in discovering splendid scenery, his struggles against appalling winter weather, his meetings with many delightful and dedicated people, his battles with injuries …

His book will appeal to all with a love for the outdoors; to those who know, or may wish to know better, the coastal regions of England, Wales, Northern Ireland, the Irish Republic and Scotland; and those who will be fascinated to learn how a relatively inexperienced walker could, with courage and an over-riding determination to succeed, overcome what seemed at times to be near-insurmountable problems.

John has agreed to donate half his royalties from sales of the book to the Multiple Sclerosis Society, an amount that will be matched by an equal contribution from the publishers.

Price £8.95. 208 pages. ISBN 1-869922-25-5. 11 photographs. Paperback. 229mm × 145mm.

From booksellers or direct from the publishers. Please send remittance plus £1.00 for postage and packing to:

Meridian Books
40 Hadzor Road • Oldbury • Warley • West Midlands • B68 9LA

Now you can walk, cycle or drive …

In the Footsteps of the Gunpowder Plotters
by Conall Boyle

You can forget about Guy Fawkes – he was just the explosives expert. The real leader of the Plot of 1605 to overthrow the Government of James the First of England was one Robert Catesby. It was he, helped by many other men of the Midlands, who hatched and executed the Plot. And not common men; the Plotters were English gentlemen of substance, owners of landed estates, some were titled, and some related to the most powerful families in the land.

Throughout 1604 Catesby schemed and plotted, bringing his accomplices up to the fateful number thirteen. These included John Grant from Northbrook, near Warwick; Ambrose Rookwood at Clopton House, close to Stratford-upon-Avon; Sir Everard Digby at Coughton Court, near Alcester; another Winter, Robert, brother of Thomas. Also involved but to a lesser extent were Stephen and Humphrey Littleton (connected with Hagley Hall).

Blowing up Parliament in London, killing the King and his two sons was to be but the first stage of the Catholic uprising. The next stages were to take place in the Midlands. Prior to the Fifth, a small army was to be assembled at Dunchurch, east of Coventry. As soon as they heard that the King was killed, the next stage of the plan would go into action – the capture of Princess Elizabeth from Coombe Abbey not far from Dunchurch. Aged nine, she would have been the remaining daughter of the King, and could be installed as the Regent, a sort of puppet monarch.

After that the main uprising would start. Houses throughout the Midlands were stockpiled with arms and gunpowder. The Plotters somewhat idealistically hoped that their little Catholic army would be joined by supporters in the Midlands, from Lancashire and from Wales, and would then go on to take power in the capital city.

But of course the Plot failed. Guy Fawkes was caught with a lighted taper and a huge quantity of gunpowder. Catesby and others got away from London and rode up to Dunchurch arriving in the evening of the fifth. The game was up; all they could do was flee from the avenging justice of the King. And so it was that a small band of desperate men set off westwards from Dunchurch, visiting many of their Houses, until eventually they were surrounded and killed or captured two days later at Holbeche House near Wolverhampton.

In this unique guide you can follow the route the Plotters took on their flight and re-live those few days in 1605. Some of the houses they called at are still there; the countryside has changed and major industrial cities have sprung up in the almost 400 years since the Plot, but a surprising amount remains.

There are three types of trip described in the book: drives by car; rides by bicycle; and walks (and most of the walks can also be done by bike). A bike is a grand way of recreating the feeling of being a fleeing Plotter, but walking is equally good.

Price £4.95. ISBN 1-869922-23-9. 96 pages. 13 drawings. 19 maps. Paperback. A5.

From booksellers or direct from the publishers. Please send remittance plus 75p. for postage and packing to:

Meridian Books
40 Hadzor Road • Oldbury • Warley • West Midlands • B68 9LA

through delightful countryside, until terminating at Chasewater reservoir. It is described in twelve sections to provide a series of walks ranging from 5¼ to 11 miles.

This fully revised and extended second edition also contains ten additional circular 'canal-link' walks covering some of the attractive walking areas adjacent to the canals.

£4.95. ISBN 1-869922-19-0. 112 pages. 31 photographs. 24 maps. Paperback. A5.

HIDDEN HEREFORDSHIRE
A Book of Country Walks
by Julie Meech

A churchyard awash with spring daffodils, a river bordered with ancient willows, a unique Norman church with comic, grotesque and erotic carvings, a fourteenth century dovecote with 666 nesting places, a Neolithic burial chamber, countless medieval timber-framed buildings, a chance to see the rare Red Kite — these are but a few of the delights encountered in this book of twenty circular walks.

£4.95. ISBN 1-869922-16-6. 112 pages. 21 photographs. 20 maps. Paperback. A5.

WATERSIDE WALKS *in the* MIDLANDS
by Birmingham Ramblers
Edited by Peter Groves

Twenty-two walks featuring brooks, streams, pools, rivers and canals, in their many aspects. Some can be found a short distance from the centre of Britain's second city; others will take the reader further afield in the West Midlands and into the attractive counties of Warwickshire, Worcestershire, Shropshire, Staffordshire and Derbyshire.

£4.95. ISBN 1-869922-09-3. 112 pages. 28 photographs. 22 maps. Paperback. A5.

LET'S WALK
by Mark Linley

A guide, illustrated with sketches and many lively cartoons, giving advice and information on clothing and equipment, walking companions, where to go, walking holidays, map and compass reading, wildlife in the countryside, leadership, difficulties and hazards, first aid, preserving the countryside, weather, and much else.

£4.95. 1988. ISBN 1-869922-03-4. 144 Pages. Paperback. A5. Illustrated with 135 sketches and cartoons.

OUT FOR THE DAY IN THE EAST MIDLANDS
by Ron Wilson

An extensive guide giving details of over seven hundred places in the counties of Leicestershire, Lincolnshire and Nottinghamshire where you can go for an enjoyable day out.

£5.95. ISBN 1-869922-21-2. 160 pages. 21 photographs. Paperback. 229mm × 145mm.

WANDERERS IN NORTHAMPTONSHIRE
Following in the steps of George Harrison, artist, writer and poet
by John and Vera Worledge

George Harrison (1876-1950) was a fine artist with a great love for the Northamptonshire countryside who travelled the county in the 1920s, '30s and '40s sketching and writing for local newspapers. John and Vera Worledge have followed in his footsteps and have combined some of George Harrison's original material with their own photographs and accounts of their visits to many of his favourite spots, so creating a series of delightful cameos of a lovely county as it is today and as it was half a century and more ago.

£4.95. ISBN 1-869922-18-2. 112 pages. 53 photographs, 73 drawings. Paperback. 229mm × 145mm.

WANDERERS IN NORTHAMPTONSHIRE:
THE SECOND JOURNEY
Following further in the steps of George Harrison, artist, writer and poet
(1876-1950)
by John and Vera Worledge
In this second volume John and Vera Worledge complete their tour of Northamptonshire and combine more of George Harrison's original material with their own photographs and accounts of visits to this attractive county.
£4.95. ISBN 1-869922-24-7. 112 pages. 53 photographs, 73 drawings. Paperback. 229mm × 145mm.

EXPLORING NORTHAMPTONSHIRE
by Tony Noble
Twenty trails, each having an historical or geographical theme, which will enable you to explore a county which is traditionally known for its 'spires and squires'. Fully illustrated with photographs and maps.
£5.95. Second Edition. ISBN 1-869922-01-8. 152 pages. 61 photographs. 24 maps. Paperback. A5.

Prices correct at 1 January 1995.
From booksellers or direct from Meridian Books. Please send remittance, adding the following amounts per book for postage and packing:
And the Road Below £1.00; *other titles* 75p

Meridian Books
40 Hadzor Road • Oldbury • Warley • West Midlands • B68 9LA
Tel: 0121-429 4397
Please send s.a.e. for our complete catalogue of books on walking and local history.

---

and for the remainder of the walk...

The Monarch's Way

Book 2
The Cotswolds, the Medips and the Sea
Stratford-upon-Avon to Charmouth
To be published Summer 1995

The Monarch's Way

Book 3
The South Coast, the Downs and Escape
In preparation